The Magic Children

The Magic Children

RACIAL IDENTITY AT THE END OF THE AGE OF RACE

Roger Echo-Hawk

Left Coast Press Inc.

Walnut Creek, CA

Left Coast Press Inc.

Left Coast Press, Inc.
1630 North Main Street, #400
Walnut Creek, CA 94596
http://www.LCoastPress.com

ISBN 978-1-59874-574-0 hardcover
ISBN 978-1-59874-575-7 paperback
eISBN 9781598745764

Library of Congress Cataloging-in-Publication Data

Echo-Hawk, Roger C.
  The magic children : racial identity at the end of the age of race /
Roger Echo-Hawk.
     p. cm.
  ISBN 978-1-59874-574-0 (hardcover : alk. paper) -- ISBN 978-1-59874-575-7
(pbk. : alk. paper)
1. Indians of North America--Ethnic identity. 2. Echo-Hawk, Roger C.--
Childhood and youth. 3. United States--Race relations. I. Title.
  E98.E85E25 2010
  305.800973--dc22
                    2010025899

Printed in the United States of America

The paper used in this publication meets the minimum requirements of AmericanNational Standard for Information Sciences—Permanence of Paper for Printed LibraryMaterials, ANSI/NISO Z39.48–1992.

The original version of Part Three, "The Haunted Statue," appeared in *Square One*, Number 2, Spring 2004, p. 46–47.

"Reflections on Repatriation, 1997" was originally published as "Reflections on Repatriation: Images of Academic America in the Mirror of NAGPRA," *The Wyoming Archaeologist*, Volume 43, Number 1, Spring 1999, p. 44–49.

Cover design by Allison Smith

Cover illustration: the cover photograph (Nebraska State Historical Society RG2078.PH1-9) was taken by William H. Jackson in September 1871. It shows Pawnee children standing in front of an earthlodge at Wild Licorice Creek, the last Pawnee metropolis in Nebraska. These unidentified children were born into a community that had for several generations embraced racial identity systems, and these children grew up thinking of themselves as "American Indians."

To the Cinnamon Girl
& all our magic circles

Contents

Preface

What Happens Next

Here at the beginning of a new millennium, a new kind of discourse about race is gradually evolving. Sustained by the findings of science, this discourse is slowly recognizing that academic scholarship rejects the idea of race as a useful description of human physical diversity. In essence, race is dead.

What does this mean?

In *The Magic Children* I suggest that whether or not individual practitioners of race choose to let go of the familiar social usages of racial identity, the world must act on this new understanding of race.

Rooted in historically false assumptions about humanity, the present-day practices of race are inherently dehumanizing because they enact a deforming narrative about the nature of humankind. In my opinion, race deserves to die. For those of us who embrace the rejection of racial identity, we must go in quest of meaningful alternatives for ourselves. We must envision some kind of a social world that permits the existence of non-racial cultural choices.

This is the conclusion I draw about the appropriate destiny of race. What is your opinion, your vision of the future of race? Powerful social forces often drive us into the future, and our destinations in life choose us as often as we choose them. But we ought to make our own introspective decisions about race and racial identity.

This fateful journey is inevitable. And it will not follow an easy path. Since racial identities take shape in our lives as strongly held belief systems, the slowly unfolding transformation of race in the world will necessarily take place as an intensely personal inner challenge.

The Magic Children is a personal account of what happened to me when I began to wrestle with race. This book ponders one form of race-based identity: racial Indianhood. But readers will readily grasp how many of my experiences translate to other racial identity systems.

Making our own choices, each of us must necessarily do alone whatever must be done. At least, that's the way I did it. Perhaps that is how it must be done.

But with this book in hand, maybe you're not really alone.

When you make your choices about race, and when you contend with what it means in your life, let me know someday what happened next.

1

In the Fifteenth Dream

& every so often in the many years that followed
my seven dreams, dreams that happened long ago
magic bears sometimes slipped inside my sleeping
in this dream Linda devised a game to get our cat
Rico, more comfortable with our hands, thrusting
her hands out of the arms of an oversized sweater
Rico found this new game very funny so I put on
a huge sweater & I surprised him with my hands
Rico likewise popped his paws out of his sweater
& as I high-fived him—both of us in a fine humor
—I realized that Rico was a bear, not a cat, & yes
he slept in wintertime and I opened a newsletter
from the National Park Service to read their wise
advice for homes like ours with hibernating bears
& as I stood turning the pages of the newsletter I
experienced a series of scenes, like memories: *Set
aside a special room in the winter. Keep it dark.
Keep the room well stocked with water and food.
Your bear will occasionally awaken to eat. Don't
be on hand when your bear awakens to eat.* Yes I
had always taken the proper steps & in the spring
when I awoke from my dream it was in the spring
of 2009, one Saturday afternoon, & I found Rocky
Rico's brother, asleep nearby… slowly awakening
I wondered: do cats ever dream about being bears?

2

Nothing Is Real

I know what it's like to have a racial identity because I used to be an Indian. Race helped to shape my earliest experience of the world. People saw me as an Indian and I learned to see myself that way and I believed in the whole concept of race. As a child, being Indian and having race felt shallow and mysterious at first, but it felt real enough. It felt important, too—it wasn't at all a slight matter to have race.

Entering adulthood, race came to mean many things that both helped and hindered my lot in life. It meant that some people would automatically accept me, while others would regard me with an impersonal curiosity and a few people would treat me with open hostility. It powerfully shaped the stories I told to myself and to others. I had race and lived it in my life. And understanding firsthand the authority and vigor and meaning of racial identity, I had no idea what to do when I discovered the truth about race.

Race tells us a lie—a lie that defaces the true nature of humanity. The idea of race has more to do with satisfying the human impulse to sort people into convenient social groupings than with providing an accurate biological definition of humankind. And the impulse of race is never benign in our world. Drawing on pseudoscience, the cultural practice of race gathers and wields a kind of social power that requires us to dehumanize ourselves and each other.

This truth may sound easily spoken, as if it ought to be self-evident. Even so, I heard it spoken for several years before I did anything about it. Thinking back, I guess the sound of it felt hesitant to me, a rumor not yet very sure of its intentions. *Race is a lie.* And perhaps the simplicity of this statement makes the whole thing sound like a simple matter. But I haven't forgotten the way I looked around at my world to see how the whole towering edifice of race took no notice; race went on in our midst. How could this whispery truth ever expect to cause even the slightest tremor among the vast truths of race, the vast utterances of racial identity?

In our world, constructions of race powerfully support both personal identity and social meaning, and the racial structures of American culture seem unambiguous, unshakeable. But if race lacks a sustaining foundation in science, what does this mean for our race-based cultural productions, our institutions of race, our laws, our social arrangements and outcomes? As a historian, this is an interesting question for me because I feel professionally curious about the stories we tell about ourselves. Since race disfigures the biological character of our humanity, surely it must also distort the cultural outcomes in our storytelling. If we were to remove the distortions, would we get more clarity about ourselves?

In the world I grew up in, people often enough asked me, *Are you Indian?* This used to be an easy and friendly conversation. I'd say *Yes, I'm Pawnee.* By this time we would be shaking hands as if race were just an amiable way to get to know people. But people don't readily get my meaning when I say that I was once an Indian and chose to give it up. It doesn't make much sense to people who believe in race. To explain myself, it seemed helpful to write this book.

In these pages I explore what it means personally that science has rejected race as a useful idea. This academic challenge to race has attracted little public notice, yet it surely means something of great consequence for us all. Thinking of what to say, I suggest that we need a new public discourse about race—one which carefully considers what the end of race-as-biology signifies for our private and public lives.

Discussion on the nature of race is mostly confined to academic circles. But since the truth about race raises a fundamental challenge to the way we've built our personal identities and our social systems, we are surely on the verge of a world that will be very different from the one we grew up in.

☉☉

In the twentieth century everyone grew up deeply rooted in the mysteries of the cult of race. I was born in 1954 as the fourth child of a "white" mother and an "Indian" father. We were all heirs of a flourishing racial belief system in America. As I entered this world, I became aware of the nature of race by encountering its various structures.

My father served in the Air Force and in the early 1960s we were stationed at Ramey Air Force Base in Puerto Rico. Driving through the racially segregated American South in January 1963, I recall being denied service in one restaurant. Arriving in Puerto Rico later that month, we fell under the label of "white," but I was once stopped by the police at Ramey because I looked too dark to be a white American. Returning to the States in 1966, we were denied access to a swimming pool in New York City due to our "color." Race riots erupted in Omaha, our new temporary home for the summer.

All the while, I puzzled over what it meant to be Indian, to be white. Somehow neither category seemed to match my situation in life, though I didn't question these racial labels. Race was something to submit to, not question.

As with most other Americans, the story of my genetic heritage is complex and not at all served by the simple tale of race. Through my parents, a very diverse set of ancestors wandered into my genetic pathways from such populations as the Pawnee (Kitkahahki, Chaui, and Pumpkin Vine Skidi), Oto (Buffalo Clan), French (French-Canadian Clan), Swiss (German-speaking Clan), English, German, Mexican, and no doubt from many other people of the world.

It does considerable violence to my complex heritage to reduce it to being "Indian" or "white" or some other awkward oversimplification of race. In the quest to refine biological theory through scientific knowledge, and in the evolution of cultural experience and social practice, race obscures more than it reveals about our humanity. It gives us a poorly edited story of ourselves.

ᱬ

Whether mostly remembered or mostly forgotten, each of us has a personal racial origin story. Mulling over my earliest memories, it would be interesting to have some distinct recollections of my sense of self as a young pre-racial child. But very little comes up; random instants and feelings.

I felt like I didn't have any toys. I recruited groups of acorns for my soldiers and I used them to enact little dramatic stories. When you knocked them over with imaginary bullets and explosions, their acorn hats would roll off just like hats in westerns on television.

I followed my mother around. Then one day I realized she found my demands wearisome; it was a stunning thought. My sister and two brothers and my father loomed over me at unpredictable moments. They performed their magic doings for me as though I might be inside a television with them.

Pondering these images, I recall my first awareness of race. The story I have always told myself hasn't faded. Perhaps it was especially memorable because it served as my first explanation for the world and how I fit in.

Talking to my mother about it in 2004, she doesn't remember the incident. She had moved on with the center of her life by the time it happened. But for me, I think of the details and they're still vivid—a little dramatic story.

ᱬ

When I was a little boy in first grade, I hurried home one day to ask my folks an important question. "Dad," I said, worried about something another kid had called me that day on the playground, "what am I, anyway?"

Mom and Dad were sitting together in our kitchen at Whiteman Air Force Base. He was a boom operator and had the rank of staff sergeant or thereabouts, and he didn't take my troubles very seriously. He had his own troubles at the time, mostly having to do with the fact that he had a family and often didn't seem to want one.

It was 1960, and things got quite heated when kids who were for Nixon began vying with kids who were for Kennedy, competing for control of the merry-go-round. I don't recall who I campaigned for. But that day somebody had tossed a slur my way, calling me a redskin. Hearing the hateful tone, I hotly denied it.

"I'm no redskin!" "You are!" "Am not!" "Redskin!" It made me want to fight him, but I thought I might first do some research on the question. I had some strong suspicions that needed to be settled.

"Well, son," Dad said, pretending to give my problem serious thought, "you're part Indian, part Mexican, and part Rebel. So I bet you can really fight if you have to." Mom chuckled a bit and chided him gently, "Oh, Walt!"

"Well, that's what he is!"

"Is not!"

"Is so!"

While they worked out what he should have said to me, I left for my room to mull things over.

I was both distressed and a little pleased. I hadn't known for sure that I was an Indian, and it didn't sit too well, what with everything I saw on TV. But it was encouraging to know that I had what it took to be a successful fighter if the need arose.

I pictured myself beating up the mean paleface kid who had called me a redskin. I pounded him mercilessly and then noticed that the girl I liked was looking on admiringly. He had been mean to her as well. And I had jumped in to get him to leave her alone.

So we fought! He wrestled me down on my bunk-bed and I threw him across the room. The fight went on all over the room in my imagination. Then I slugged him several times with my tough little Indian fists and pretty soon I found myself holding hands with my new girlfriend, whispering to her, kissing her—this would be my first kiss that really mattered.

What came next? I didn't exactly know. What I saw on TV wasn't too clear on this point, but I would know what to do when the moment arrived.

I lay on my bed, thinking. That paleface kid had been right. I was an Indian after all. How had he known? Did I look like an Indian? I didn't think so.

I tried to sort things out.

Dad's an Indian; Mom is white . . . where did the Mexican come in? Mom didn't look Mexican and Dad was an Indian. Maybe Dad had just been joking about that. Maybe he was simply teasing me, saying that I looked like a Mexican or acted like one in some way. Would this be a problem for me? I was no Mexican!

But I had been wrong about not being a redskin. Maybe it would turn out that I was somehow Mexican. Anyway, they were all good fighters. That's what really mattered.

Okay, so I looked something like an Indian . . . but I really wanted to look like Elvis! One of my classmates was a handsome kid with red hair, and he could comb his hair just like Elvis. One time that girl I liked pushed him down on the ground and kissed him. I made friends with him, and he took me and another fellow into the bathroom to show us how to comb our hair like his, like Elvis. But my hair refused to cooperate with this plan and I never looked like Elvis.

In the end, my research project left me with lots of questions.

But I didn't ever fight that paleface kid, and I never did anything heroic and I never got to kiss that girl I liked. Elvis got drafted into the Army right around that time and cut his hair and then made some movies. Kennedy finally won the merry-go-round competition.

Every so often during the decades that followed I thought about the mysteries of race and how I fit in. When middle-age materialized around me, I resumed my research project. Scholars in anthropology and biology, I discovered, had been challenging the idea of race for a long time and there now seemed to be a fairly uniform set of opinions among them.

Studying this literature, I learned that there's nothing to support the idea of race as a biological reality. As the eminent geneticist Luigi Luca Cavalli-Sforza explains to his son, Francesco, in *The Great Human Diasporas*: "The idea of race in the human species serves no purpose."

This sums up very nicely what I discovered in my research. It came as a bit of a shock when I thought about what it meant, and it took some time for me to decide to give up being Indian, to work on not seeing people in racial terms. Being "Mexican" is a matter of national citizenship, and I'm not a citizen of Mexico.

So I'm not Indian, white, or Mexican. That leaves me with being a rebel.

I guess I'm a bit of a rebel.

☾☽

In my Missouri childhood we occasionally packed up our paper bag "suitcases" and set forth to visit Pawnee, Oklahoma. It took eight or nine hours to drive to Pawnee, but our arrival was always mysterious to me because my father wandered down different routes into town and I could never figure out how we got there. We'd be driving along in the dark, and just as dawn crept up to surprise the world, I would see a completely unexpected angle on the town.

I don't know how many times we made that trip. It was just something that happened every so often. Those experiences no doubt provided me with some of the fundamental notions of selfhood that grew into my racial identity, but the idea of race must have grown slowly in my world. I don't remember exactly when I learned how to do race.

If you have children you'll help to teach them about race. You'll go around living race and your kids will see you living it and they'll pick it up gradually. You might go further and teach them specific things about what it means to have race and what it means to encounter other people who have a different race.

My father used to say, "You have to get along with colored people, and this is important because you might have to work with them someday—but you don't have to be friends with them!" His father had been involved in the Ku Klux Klan during the Great Depression. In my grandfather's world, my dad learned to tolerate "colored people" as a lower form of humankind, ranked just above the Sioux. My father and his father believed in race and embraced the view that "coloreds" couldn't help their condition, but the Sioux had no excuse whatsoever.

My dad's racist attitudes seemed obscure to me because his fatherhood occurred in my life more as a set of performances than as a sustained and involved presence. When I grew up and became a hippie and a bit of a rebel, I found it was easy to reject the things he believed about race.

In my personal origin stories I saw the rise of the youth counterculture of the late 1960s and I took part, but I had no reason to doubt the doing of race. I had no reason to question the idea of being Indian. I didn't know that race wasn't real. I didn't know that it was only something invented by other people.

ൟ

Every so often I come up with an idea for a new invention, and I say to my wife: "Linda, if you were a real engineer, you'd make a million bucks with this!" She's a software engineer and I don't have any idea what she does.

One day I came up with a great idea for a rather important purpose, but I quickly realized that it would take a little science and a little engineering to make it work. It has to do with the way we understand race. My idea for an invention would help to change the way we see ourselves and other people. The problem is that I don't have any clue about how to make it work.

I'm not much of a scientist. I was a teenager in the early 1970s when I designed my one and only actual science experiment. I noticed that when I dropped acid and mescaline the wallpaper in my room upstairs would slowly flow downward late at night. This interested me greatly and it's still a mystery.

On each such occasion this steady and mysterious motion happened exactly the same way. The wallpaper designs wouldn't actually move, of course. Something like an invisible plastic covered everything with a beautiful semblance of motion. I tried different things to see if I could speed it up or slow it down: turning off the light, squinting, moving my head about quickly, but this magic sheath always moved at the same graceful rate everywhere in the room.

One day I wrote some poems around the door frame, thinking that the next time I tripped I would see whether the words flowed with the invisible plastic. I hypothesized that it would be quite interesting to watch the poetry flow down the wall. And I envisioned myself hurrying downstairs in a white lab coat to watch as the words continued slipping down into the earth under the house. It would have been very cool, I thought, to live in a house that floated on a pool of moving poetry.

But before I could test this hypothesis, my father made me scrub off the poetry. "When you get your own house," he said to me, peering with a hostile critic's eye at what I had written, "you can write whatever you like on the walls."

I blame my father for the fact that I never invented anything useful and I never became a scientist. If it weren't for him, maybe we would all be living in houses with fabulously interesting wallpaper.

Anyway, having talked to a lot of people over the years about race and what it means that the idea of race has no valid biological justification, I know this mostly leaves people mystified and confused and even a little angry.

It's as though I had told a story in which the explanatory parts were in Latin.

I know what this is like, having read such stories in George Dorsey's *Traditions of the Skidi Pawnee.* In one such story, told by an old man named White Eagle, Coyote meets a raccoon next to a stream of water and asks, "Num tecum ludere licet, nepos meus?" They go on at length in Latin and it's hilarious.

Latin is okay for scientists, I understand, but everyone knows that it's really the best language for salacious stuff about animals with funny sexual habits. I took Latin in high school back in the early 1970s, and Mr. Farris was a fascinating teacher even though he couldn't tell stories like old man White Eagle could.

Most people seem to grasp very readily the story that science tells about race, about how race is a bogus concept founded on old-fashioned pseudoscience that has long been debated and discredited by biologists, geneticists, and anthropologists. But I have discovered that it is nevertheless quite a lot of trouble to get those same people to consider what this means. I sometimes suspect that it would be far simpler if someone just invented a liquid that could be surreptitiously sprayed on people, relieving them suddenly of their much-treasured but false notions about race.

This would come in handy when the talk gets around to complicated words that sound like Latin, such as "epistasis" and "pleiotropy." These words are actually Greek terms having to do with highly technical genetic effects, and I don't use them, but I've seen them being used. One of my favorite authors is Joseph L. Graves Jr., and he uses words like these in explaining why people—especially clinicians—suppose that race is real. I picture a bunch of doctors giggling at the hilarious things that happen when organisms do weird stuff at the genetic level.

It would be far easier, in my opinion, when dealing with obstinate clinicians, to toss out some Latin and Greek terms, and while they're throwing their heads back chuckling at the absurd and somewhat salacious imagery, to swiftly and secretly dose them with your de-race atomizer, hidden in your sleeve. Then a few moments after it kicks in, ask something like, "What were you just saying about hypertension in black people?"

They would look blankly at you, "Black people? What do you mean by that, anyway?"

This would help immensely in the effort to get people on track with what human biological diversity really consists of, and what this means for the ways we have shaped our society. To be sure, it would be rude to take away the ability of people to make personal decisions about race. But I have noticed that racialists don't really believe that people ought to have a choice about the doing of race, so it might be fun—even if somewhat callous—to treat them like they themselves don't deserve a choice about giving it up.

To add to the fun, a really callous inventor could make a special attachment that would introduce a bit of acid or mescaline into the mix. When I think of this, I picture us all living in houses that float on poetry.

ඛා

As my various origin stories recede from the walls of my present into the past, the details slip away slowly, gently. But I can still point to one specific day when I said, yes, I'm an Indian. This sounds more definitive than it really is, because I grew up thinking *I'm an Indian*. Even though this seemed a solid foundation for selfhood, I had little idea what it really meant. There wasn't any emotional depth to the feeling. It was just something I couldn't deny.

Yes, I'm an Indian.

But a subtle change occurred one day in the late summer of 1973.

When I was 18 in the spring of 1973 I had three close friends: Dennis Smith, Mark Beelek, and Jerri Hof. Together we invented a plan. We would buy a car and drive to a distant forest at the edge of the known world—Basin, Montana—and we would become ourselves together.

But my oldest brother suggested an alternative. Come out here to Boulder, he suggested, and I'll help you get into school. My brother was an Indian and he had recently graduated from law school and he had gotten a job at the Native American Rights Fund (NARF) in Boulder, Colorado. One of our cousins had helped to found NARF just a few years earlier. It was an Indian law firm and they practiced Indian law.

I pondered the thought of moving to Colorado. I didn't really want to go to college. But I wanted to be a writer. Maybe I could do that as a student. After talking it over with my friends, I decided to go to Boulder. Jerri agreed to come with me, and in the summer of 1973 we took the bus to Colorado. Moving into a little efficiency apartment in Boulder, I became a student at the University of Colorado.

My brother suggested that I pay a visit to the Indian Educational Opportunity Program office to look for funding. This Indian EOP office was located in a basement just around the corner from NARF.

One day I headed over there and walked down three or four steps and opened the door and pretty soon I found myself in a chair looking at the woman who ran the program. She glanced toward me in a friendly way across her cluttered desk.

I sat quietly in her office. I was a hippie, not an Indian, but she thought I was an Indian and she would find me some money to go to school.

In the midst of this social reality, the phone on her desk rang. Most people are happily enslaved to their phones. And no matter what might be happening in the immediate world, if it rings they'll rush to answer. Her hand moved nonchalantly through the air and she picked up the phone, obedient.

"Well, hello!" She said to the phone. It had mastered her and she felt delighted. "How are you!" The phone spoke to her in its tiny, commanding voice; I politely tried not to listen. It asked her what she was doing.

"Oh, I'm just sittin' here lookin' at a handsome young Indian guy!" A handsome young Indian guy. . . .

She winked at me, trying to put me at ease as she conversed with her plastic telephone.

Okay, I'm an Indian. I'll agree with her about that and I'll get money to be an Indian at CU. I'll write poetry and be a hippie—no, an *Indian*— poet. It won't help me to talk about being a hippie and to speak of my origin stories as a hippie. No one cares about that in the world of college funding sources.

I left the Indian EOP office and walked back to my apartment. I had long hair and I was a . . . a handsome young Indian guy. I walked slowly across the university through a pleasantly sunny now-long-vanished summer day. I followed a winding path that angled down a bluff into a narrow forest along Boulder Creek.

Jerri stood there in our new apartment on Folsom Street. "Well," she looked at me with her green eyes. "How did it go?"

I didn't know what I should make of racial Indianhood just yet. But while I was gone that afternoon, I had become a handsome young Indian.

We smiled at one another. It didn't matter to her who I was beyond that room. We were poor young hippies and we loved each other and race didn't matter very much to us. In our apartment with her I was just myself.

But out in the world I would thenceforth be an Indian student at CU. No one would ever give me money to be a hippie and go to college—the world funded my sense of racial Indianhood. Race shaped my identity as a student.

My years with Jerri Hof unfolded and the 1970s came to an end and we went our separate ways. During the 1970s I wasn't much of an adherent to the practice of racial Indianhood, but I didn't make any effort to avoid race. During the 1980s I took it up in my life, and by the end of the 1990s I had begun to give it up. When the new century opened at the beginning of the new millennium, I found myself back where I started.

If I rented that same little apartment in Boulder and went back to college again, who would I be this time?

3

The Haunted Statue

I n my origin stories I became a hippie in my youth, not an Indian. Being Indian certainly mattered, but no one held me to it—my friends weren't particularly concerned with my race and I didn't make it a priority. Trying to imagine what things might feel like without race, I naturally think of that time; I go back to my origin stories as a hippie.

By the late 1960s the civil rights movement had been largely successful in putting racism on the defensive as a force in American life. Race had been wielded to ensure white privilege, but now it could be wielded by every racial group. The pluralism of equal rights would soon take shape as multiculturalism—the peaceful coexistence of fully empowered races.

My experience with race in my youth was to observe the cultural shifting of the idea of race away from a position of immutable social authority and into the realm of things to challenge, to question, to change. I stood there in the late 1960s and early 1970s and pondered what it meant, but I didn't ever think that race could be denied.

A variety of cultural factors came into play to help me invent my identity as a hippie, and there was no mystical foundation of pseudobiology, as there is with racialism. There's nothing biological about being a hippie.

I listened to music, traded ideas with friends, took drugs, read books, and I became a writer. I wrote poetry and short prose, writing my first book-length manuscript in high school. Drugs, sex, and rock & roll were not the only things on our minds when I became a hippie.

I read whatever was popular at the time. Tolkien and Lord Dunsany were my favorite authors during the late 1960s. Then the writings of Richard Brautigan began floating around Jefferson City, Missouri, in 1970–1971, and my sister gave me a hardcover trilogy of Brautigan's works as a gift in December 1971. I read his books and stories and poetry with great interest and amusement.

A few years into the 1970s Brautigan published a novel called *The Hawkline Monster: A Gothic Western*. In this book, a woman temporarily imagines that she's an Indian named Magic Child, and she hires two hit men to deal with a horrid light that lives in a jar of chemicals. The hit men eventually defeat the monstrous light—they are aided in this endeavor by a pleasant little shadow that hovers around the jar of evil chemicals. But in the chapters before this battle, Brautigan has Magic Child suddenly awaken from her delusion of racial identity, which turns out to have been a spell laid upon her by the Hawkline monster.

Like Magic Child, I used to think that I was an Indian.

The world was filled with magic children, living in America under the spell of race. But one day I learned that racial identity was just something to imagine about myself, and I devoted several years of careful thought on the matter. Then shortly before that century turned into this one, before the old millennium became a young one, I decided to give it up.

It wasn't very complicated to do, but it wasn't easy either. In the tales I tell of that time, it seems pleasantly ironic that in one of them I summon up fictional characters from a book by Richard Brautigan to help defeat the fiction of race.

☙

In my library in Colorado early one morning in December 2003, I noticed that we had two copies of *The Hawkline Monster*. A hardback and a paperback. I try to recall what motivated me to get two copies of this book back in the 1970s when it was first published. But it turns out that my wife Linda had a copy when we met, and when we got together, the two books found one another and have not parted since. At one time or another, I've had many of Brautigan's books. Just a few have accompanied me into the present, including these two copies of *The Hawkline Monster*.

In the early 1970s, writing my first book in high school, I didn't know the truth about the lie of race, but I did know about Richard Brautigan. Brautigan exerted a powerful influence on me. I still have a rather jumbled copy of my first book in a box in my office. Looking at this manuscript in late 2003, I realized suddenly what an impact Brautigan had on me as a young writer. Weak echoes of Brautigan appeared everywhere in the poetry and prose, though completely lacking his genius, his wise humor, and all the magically fragile angles that invite us into his sidelong version of the mundane world.

I never thought *The Hawkline Monster* really measured up to his earlier work, but I liked it a great deal more than *Willard and His Bowling Trophies*. Readers who started off with *Willard* got cheated if they felt inclined at all to set this Richard Brautigan fellow aside forever. On the other hand, I don't recall anything specific about *Willard*, and maybe now I would enjoy it more than I did all those years ago.

Anyway, by the end of the 1970s, I had set aside the writings of Richard Brautigan and had moved on. When that decade gave way to the 1980s, I became an Indian in Boulder, Colorado, and I had a good time being an Indian and I'm glad those days happened.

The new decade started off pretty well for me because I lived with my oldest brother and then with my sister and they had excellent social skills and both were popular and active members of the Boulder Indian community. I hung around with them and looked over their shoulders as they went about doing the things they did in that world.

In those days we didn't wrestle with the idea of being Indian. Nor did we have a choice about being Indian like we do nowadays. Whether or not we liked being Indian, the story we told about it was that for most Indians it wasn't easy being Indian. For most Indians maybe it was good to be Indian, but it was too often needlessly difficult because of white racism. So it was the mission of our community in Boulder to make things generally better for Indian people everywhere, to help ease the crushing legacy of insensitive white oppression.

My oldest brother was an Indian lawyer at the Native American Rights Fund in Boulder, and my sister was an Indian student at the University of Colorado, Boulder campus. NARF and CU together made the Boulder Indian community what it was in that time. I took part in various interesting things that happened there during the 1980s—things like the annual *Ken Springer Memorial Basketball Tournament*, a tournament for Indian basketball teams, and *Visions of the Earth*, the annual NARF art show for Indian artists and Indian artwork.

It was very satisfying being involved in the local Indian scene in Boulder, Colorado, with warm socializing at a succession of favored bars. And there were plenty of parties and other events that brought the local crowd together. And as the 1980s wore on, it turned out to be just as much fun to be an Indian while working at NARF. This national law firm did important work for Indian tribes in Indian country in the area of federal Indian law, improving things here and there for Indians.

Although this work was a serious thing to do, I enjoyed doing it because I'd become the NARF copy coordinator/mail clerk and it was often pretty fun to do that and to be an Indian during the late 1980s in Boulder. We felt like we were taking part in something very special at NARF. We helped Indians and their Indian tribal governments in their battles against social injustice, and it felt good to do the worthwhile things we did.

I was also a writer during the 1980s—an Indian writer. And I had a lot of fun when one day early in the decade I suddenly became the correspondent on Indian affairs for a Boulder literary newspaper called *Rolling Stock*, edited by two of Richard Brautigan's friends, Jenny Dorn and her husband Ed.

I didn't care then that the editors of *Rolling Stock* gave me that opportunity because I was an Indian. I felt like I was part of something special at *Rolling Stock*. It was a privilege to ride along in its excursions beyond the beaten track of the literary world, and it gives me a warm feeling to think of it.

Then during the late 1980s I went back to college and became an Indian student at the University of Colorado, Boulder campus. I studied history and anthropology and took courses that had to do with racial Indianhood, and I learned a lot of very interesting things about how race had been done historically, and about how race should be done even better.

I think back with a glow of pleasure to those days because the 1980s were often fun for Indians if you happened to be an Indian, as I was, in Boulder, Colorado. Whatever other people experienced elsewhere during the 1980s, for me it was a great time to be an Indian and I'm glad I did it.

Since I feel happy when I think of being Indian during that decade, maybe it would be easy to just accept that having been an Indian, it was a good thing because it felt nice for me emotionally. When I think of what it was like to be an Indian during the 1980s in Boulder, I might logically conclude that race can be a positive thing.

In fact, I met people who wished to be Indian but couldn't ever be Indian. They looked at those of us who were Indian and they knew they wanted to be Indian, too, because being Indian was something special. Did I ever feel that way myself? Like I might be special, being Indian? Maybe. Yes. No. The problem for me was that I knew what it was like already to participate in something special, and this racial way of feeling special somehow felt different.

I'd been pretty happy as a hippie. It had been a lot of fun finding interesting ways to expand my mind. Cultivating an ethic of open-mindedness about cultural experience, when the 1980s dawned I thought it might be interesting to take up being an Indian. This seemed logical enough since I was a member of an Indian family, a citizen of an Indian tribe.

Thinking back to the things I did as an Indian, in a small way I see how I helped the next generation of adherents to racial Indianhood to understand what it meant to be an Indian and to have race. Like Brautigan's Magic Child, I believed in racial identity and I did my part in handing along race. As another magic child, I helped to create the next generation of magic children.

I thought racial Indianhood was a good thing at the time. But whether or not it was a good thing, one day in the turmoil and quiet of the 1990s I gave it up. The 1990s came down relentlessly on the heels of the 1980s and brought an end to it all. Everyone hurtled on through that decade to the end of the century at the end of the millennium.

Now it's over. I'm not Indian anymore.

When I gave up race and started challenging it, it wasn't easy. I found myself saying stuff that came off to people like *Willard and His Bowling Trophies.*

So several years later in this next version of my life, I suddenly find myself standing in my library in December 2003 staring at my two copies of *The Hawkline Monster*. I'm thinking about getting rid of the paperback to make room for something else. I take it down. A moment later I put it back. It's certainly not one of my favorites, but now it seems very hard to banish this slight novel.

Maybe I'll keep the book and give it to my nephew someday. He's a young writer and artist, Young Bunk.

I remember when Young Bunk had green muscles.

This happened when he lived in Lyons, Colorado, in a house perched just above the shore of the St. Vrain River. He must have been age six or so. He had some plastic green Incredible Hulk muscles and he'd put them on and he would squeeze a pump hidden in one hand and the muscles would inflate. I picture him with his arms flung out like a monstrously strong little man, inflating his muscles.

Everyone thought it was hilarious and a little precocious, the way he'd expertly pose and work the secret pump and the air would whuff-whuffwhuff into the muscles and it was very entertaining because he'd play the David Banner role to the hilt, a tragic character doomed to wander the earth doing good deeds and seeking inner peace through science, having been sadly warped by good-science-gone-bad.

It was entertaining indeed to see the whole performance. Everyone would bask in the warm good humor when Young-Bunk-David-Banner became a dangerous little green Hulk. When I think back, I enjoy the way my brother and his wife laugh in my memory when their magic child performed his feat with a droll comic-book look in his eyes.

The idea of race arose like the Hulk from good-science-gone-bad. And like Richard Brautigan's Magic Child, I used to think that I was an Indian back when I believed in race, back when I first read *The Hawkline Monster* and when David Banner wandered the prime-time earth.

But being Indian was just something to imagine about myself, and after several years of careful thought on the matter, one day in the late 1990s I finally gave it up. Brautigan has Magic Child transform out of her racial identity by changing clothes and walking around a kitchen with her twin sister—the persona of "Magic Child" turns out to have been just a prank played by the Hawkline monster.

It's definitely not normal to deliberately abandon racial identity, as I have done. If I treat race like something roughly equivalent to a spell devised by a monster made of light, living in a jar of chemicals in a novel, well, I know race is much more than a prank easily shed. It might well be a biological fiction, and this view of race might well be widely accepted among experts in human biology, but to speak of this is to murmur like a little shadow before the awful lights of our enchanted world.

I have the impression that Young Bunk's Indian identity is very strong. He grew up treasuring racial Indianhood and as an artist he wields it like a spotlight in his artwork to illuminate the things he wants to say to the rest of us. And he's in good company with all the other millions of magic children of our time.

☉☉

Young Bunk,

I thought you might be interested in reading a story I wrote a couple months ago called "The Haunted Statue." I showed it to a friend of mine, Jenny Dorn, who edits a literary journal and she wants to publish it. The story mentions you and I hope you don't mind. It's about when I met Richard Brautigan in the summer of 1980 when I was a few years younger than you are now.

I was living with your family then in Boulder or at Indian Gap. You were age five that summer.

You might be interested to know that I have something you wrote then, written the same month that I met Richard—maybe the first thing you ever wrote. It's a page of markings that look like writing, but it's impossible to decipher. Your sister Amy or cousin Corby wrote your name on the envelope and you gave it to me, and I still have it all these years later. Anyway, let me know what you think about the story.

Uncle Roger
February 27, 2004

☉☉

It was my good fortune to meet Richard Brautigan in August 1980, four years before he shot himself. He had come to Boulder at the invitation of Ed and Jenny Dorn. They had arranged for him to spend an afternoon with several younger writers in Boulder, and when I mentioned that I was a fan, they very kindly included me in the group. We visited with

Richard and his new girlfriend for several hours at someone's house. My friend Wayne Moore attended and several others.

Richard spent the time relating droll stories about little things that had happened to him and his girlfriend—a woman he had just met in Boulder. He was vastly entertained by her and kept urging her to tell a certain story again and again. Something about being shown a Confederate sword and her funny reaction to it, offering to slice a roast with it. I picture her demonstrating several times how she had held the sword up over her head.

෧෨

One evening in 2004 I sat in a bookstore and read most of a book by Richard Brautigan's daughter, Ianthe. *You Can't Catch Death* is her beautifully written and very touching account of her relationship with her father.

One story she told in those pages has stuck with me. She recalled how her father used to say that when he was a child he felt afraid of statues because he thought there were actual people trapped inside them, imprisoned somehow in the cold metal.

Thinking of how he must have pictured a horrible truth, the story of how living people can become inanimate statues, I suddenly realize that something like this arguably happens to people when they get captured by race. They grow up doing everyday things and they don't care much about race until they get to be about the age Young Bunk was when he wrote his first story and when he donned his green muscles.

Kids live around people like me—like I once was when I believed in race—and they gradually get bronzed by the blinding ensnaring light of race. The first thin layers of it get cooked onto them like skin by the things we adults do and the ways we enact race.

It's a very devious process because most people don't notice and if they do, they don't mind. Maybe they feel it growing upon their surfaces like a set of very entertaining inflatable muscles. And someday the bad science of race will clasp them tight and endow them with tremendous strength and eventually they'll become fearfully implacable greenish bronze-skinned statues with real people trapped inside.

෧෨

Trapped inside my statue all those years ago, living with my siblings and their families and being Indian, it didn't feel wrong to me. So I know that being Indian doesn't feel like a lie. Race doesn't feel horrid or blinding or loathsome or like a trap.

It feels natural and the rules feel normal.

The vast majority of racialists today do their best to enact their racial identities with dignity, pride, and a sense of responsibility for doing it well. So for me to describe the initiation of racial identity as "a very devious process"—this must understandably sound unsettling, offensive even.

Caught up in my opposition to race, I suddenly pause to consider. . . . Rejecting race and critiquing the assumptions of racialists, to what degree have I also accommodated a growing insensitivity toward the people who choose to do race? Have I slowly become unable to empathize with even their highest aspirations, the most redeeming elements of their social idealism?

Whatever my own shortcomings as an anti-race non-racial ideologue, still, I argue that race is a new cultural identity system which doesn't add clarity to our understanding of the nature of humankind. Race hasn't come down to us out of the unknown mists of time. Racial Indianhood has a history, and the very idea of being Indian wasn't dreamed up first by the hallowed ancestors of contemporary adherents to racial Indianhood.

Scholars know that the technical structures of modern-day racialism were born in Europe during the eighteenth century. A German academician named Johann Blumenbach played a crucial role in defining race, and he accomplished this through the study of human skulls. Johann Herder was another German scholar of the period who helped to transform a somewhat random stew of ideas into what we recognize as race. I don't have any firsthand experience of how the Germans today do race, but it is indisputable that the doing of race is an inherently German thing to do. This is a key component of the history behind the logic of racial Indianhood.

The notion of being Indian is a new thing with a shallow past, but what matters to practitioners is the way it has become tradition. It feels very much like something that grew out of indigenous time immemorial, not like something born in eighteenth century Europe and the principalities of Germany and imposed via the processes of conquest and colonialism.

Like I said, race is devious.

Anyway, even if racial Indianness felt like the new thing that it really is, I'd guess that most Indians believe that to be an American in the twenty-first century, one must do race, and Indians don't mind being modern. Indians don't need a reason to be complicated. Indians don't want to justify their lives to anyone.

I know this is the story that magic children Indian people tell themselves and each other. And maybe it will indeed go on exactly like that for generation after generation until the misty end of time immemorial.

When I was an Indian I appreciated being part of something that felt good, like something to treasure. So when I gaze upon that world from afar I know how Indians see themselves as wanderers of the earth doing good deeds here & there.

And I sometimes sense that I have so little presence now in their doings in that whole vast world, I might as well be a little oblique shadow bending before brilliant lights.

ଚୢ

My friend Wayne Moore and I gave Richard Brautigan and his girlfriend a ride in my Subaru back to the Hotel Boulderado—the two of them like giants in the tiny back seat, busy amusing one another at things going by. I don't recall her name, but for me, in that time, she was an Asian woman riding in a car with an Indian and two white guys. I suppose this scene must still look that way to most observers all these years later.

Pulling up to the hotel, I thanked Richard for writing his books, or so I tell myself now. I can't really remember anything I said that afternoon.

I recall more clearly that when we made our farewells, Richard put his hands together and gave a gracious little bow there on the sidewalk next to the Boulderado. And somehow—just in my mind, I suppose—he lingered in that pose as Wayne and I drove off into the city.

Several years later, driving by the Boulderado after he shot himself in California, I glanced over to where I had left him, as if to look for him, affixed to the sidewalk like a statue toppling slowly for years: Richard Brautigan with a little smile, bowing forever before the strangely baffling lights that haunt the world.

4

The Bear Enchantments

The Enchanted Monkey

I have always thought that my bear dreams mattered in some mystical way. I don't recall my first awareness of them, the magic bears that suddenly took to wandering around in my head during the night. It started in early 1975, and as the year unfolded it became a regular thing, dreaming about bears. Most of these dreams slipped away immediately, but some of them came with me into the waking world. By June 1976 I had experienced what I began calling "the seven dreams."

The special bear-moments in my sleep sometimes seemed ominous and dangerous. Many were hauntingly beautiful. All felt deeply mysterious. Every so often I would awaken with the dream sequence powerfully fresh in my mind, and I'd take time to run over the scenes, to replay the strange images and events. I knew these dreams signified something, but what?

I finally confided in my cousin Bryce Wildcat. Bryce worked as some kind of researcher at the Native American Rights Fund. Getting to know him in 1970, I thought of him as a quintessential hippie, an exemplar of hippie idealism, generous and good-humored. Now here he was in Boulder, Colorado, and he helped to make this city a friendly place for me and my girlfriend Jerri.

Listening with a serious air, Bryce seemed to think I should take my bear dreams and use them to become more Indian. "It probably means something," he suggested, "you should talk to an Indian doctor about those dreams." Sure, I thought, it does seem like something having to do with being an Indian, to dream about bears.

At that point in my life, however, I didn't feel very Indian—I saw myself as a hippie. I was a student in the new creative writing program at the University of Colorado, a hippie poet. But I didn't write any poems about those dreams because I knew my writing abilities needed a lot more work and I didn't want to put these special dreams into mediocre poetry.

In the fall of 1976 I wrote down the most memorable of my bear dreams. These became my "seven dreams." In the years since that time I have had hundreds of dreams about bears. Periods happen in which I don't encounter any bears. But I always sense them lingering somewhere nearby, my magic bears, sleeping in the winter woods at the edge of my mind. I like having them in my life even if I don't know what to say about them.

I've never liked the idea that the most appropriate fate for these particular dreams should be for them to get subjected to analysis as purely symbolic psychological manifestations of my inner self. I'm not really opposed to this idea—it just seems too limited. I have the feeling that dreams most often represent something more than a kind of psychic shadow cast by the conscious mind into the night. The messy strangeness and inexplicable power of the dreamscape has too much magic to be confined to the private stage of idiosyncratic psycho-theater.

So what do I think my dreams signify?

This is not an easy question to answer. Mulling over my bear dreams one day in 2006, I realized that I hadn't ever delved very far into my vague ideas, attitudes, feelings, presumptions, guesses, and general storytelling on the topic of dreams. Deciding at last to invest some energy and time in studying the literature on dreams, I took a very casual approach in setting up my research design. I spent a few minutes perusing some likely shelves at a local bookstore. Fortunately, a convenient resource came ready to hand, and one that, quite frankly, looked edgy in its thinking without pushing too far beyond the fringe. I bought a copy of Fred Alan Wolf's *The Dreaming Universe*.

The book's subtitle promised me "a mind-expanding journey into the realm where psyche and physics meet." Okay; I'm ready. I hoped I'd catch a glimpse of the hitherto unequationed secrets of the spiritual world, the metaphysical invisibilities that really shape the physical world, the parapsychology hidden behind the psychology. The book held forth hope of the kind of self-discovery that could well yield some magic bears.

But it proved disappointing. The portions of the book that made the most convincing arguments turned me back toward the dynamics of human psychology. If the universe dreams, to know what it dreams and how its dreams relate to my dreams, we must rely solely upon imagination. In other words, Fred Alan Wolf didn't help me to sense the mystical source of the far-off growling I'd been hearing for the last thirty years—the growling of magic bears. To be sure, *The Dreaming Universe* contains quite a lot of fascinating scholarly thinking and guesswork about what dreams are made of.

In any case, for the moment I must be content with exploring what my untested unscholarly attitudes might be about dreams, my dreams. To start with, back in the late 1970s I accepted the general proposition that my bear dreams might have something to do with racial identity. The idea of a dream seemed a purely biological manifestation to me then, and so did the notion of race.

∽∾

When I became an Indian I did it by becoming a Pawnee Indian. I didn't talk to any Indian medicine people about my bear dreams, but I did think about what I was now learning about Pawnee spiritual traditions. In 1988 when I began to help my oldest brother with his labors in Pawnee and Indian repatriation, I thought I had some idea about what my bear dreams signified. I had the idea that it all had something to do with healing. With social justice.

The doing of this social-justice healings ... it wouldn't be me doing it; it would instead be the doings of the bears that visited my unconscious mind. Perhaps they wanted me to stand next to my brother so they could invisibly help him do what he did. I would have no essential responsibility in this matter. I merely had to be on hand every so often while my brother went about changing and fixing the broken world, aided by the magic bears that growled in my sleep.

I said very little to him about this. Suspecting that I had embraced a vaguely New Age way of being Indian, I knew that most real Indians didn't approve of New Age Indians, and my results-oriented practical lawyer brother was a real Indian. To speak too much of the mystical edge of my thinking about my dreams would have been pointless.

More importantly, to insert my dreams into my brother's difficult tasks would seem too self-aggrandizing, like I might believe I was somehow essential. In fact, my brother did quite well in his career without any noticeable help from me and my New Age Indian magic bears.

Another notion lingered in my mind. I had the foreboding impression that my conscious doings in the outer world would come to very little in my lifetime. I would not prove very successful in enacting any of my public performances in the conscious world, the world that takes shape from historical process. If I succeed at all in pursuing my own desires, I will succeed most when our paths converge, my conscious path and the unconscious path of the bears.

I've never felt very thrilled about this impression. I most definitely want to succeed in whatever I choose to do myself. I would quite approve if I were to look into the mirror of public acclaim and find a famous poet, a respected historian, a much-loved musician, an artist of some renown. People would encounter my doings and feel moved to thank me and give me lots of money and an occasional prestigious award.

Sometimes I told myself another related truth that seemed to come from the bears. I said to myself that even though I might never myself really succeed, anyone who tried to interfere with me directly (and here the thought becomes a little disturbing), well, maybe something would happen to get them out of the way. I'd keep going no matter what. This mysterious inward presence, the presence of the magic bears, this was the implacable reality that mattered when it came to Roger Echo-Hawk. People who tried to stop Roger Echo-Hawk would encounter something other than Roger Echo-Hawk. . . .

This is an awful thing to think, revealing more psychology than parapsychology at work in my mind. It hints at something cruel, something selfish lurking inside me—but sometimes I have believed it. When I think about it, I always feel sorry if this is true, if the bears stand guard over me. Would people really suffer because they were foolish enough to make my life a little difficult? If the bears stood ready to punish my enemies, how would I feel seeing people suffer, knowing their suffering came from the hidden forces that surround me?

Pondering such mysteries, I tell myself that I must guard against acting on any vindictive impulses—if the bears act, that is their business, not mine. Even so, whatever my beliefs in this regard, when I look into my heart, I often find myself hoping that the bears will take care of me and aid me and defend me in their invisible realm. But I don't feel very good when I suspect that the bears may sometimes harm people around me.

Still, in my bear dreams I think the bears feel everything I feel. They suffer and endure and they feel joy and pleasure. They sometimes have unknowable purposes.

Intellectually speaking, I know that I'm on my own in the world; I must find my own ways to cope with rejection, with any personal defeat that gets aimed at me. But emotionally speaking, what will the bears do? Will they intervene or decline to intervene? Are they immune to what I feel, to what I wish for?

I suppose that what matters is that I have stood here and there in the world and many interesting things have happened. In most of my sayings when I set forth my life, I don't mention my magic bears. But somewhere deep inside this is what really happened: *He dreamed of magic bears and they did the inscrutable things that had to happen.*

These thoughts took me through the rest of the twentieth century. I did what had to be done in those days, and that period is a meaningful part of my life even if it wasn't always easy. In the end, whatever I did then, many interesting things happened during the 1980s and the 1990s. I am content with the poems I have written, the history I have studied, the music I have composed.

In the next part of my life in the next century, in the next millennium, I would do the next thing in my life and the bears would . . . do what? They hadn't ever let me in on whatever it was they were bent on doing in their invisible world. There would be no reason for them to consult with me. Maybe our paths would cross every so often. I would help them at times. Sometimes they would help me.

☉☉

In 2006 I saw a psychologist talking on a television news program. I don't recall her name, but she talked about dreams and what scholarship has to say about the subject. I like to hear what other people make of dreams. I want to keep my mind open to seeing things I might never see myself.

She said she saw a worldwide pattern of dreaming among young men who have emotionally intense interactions with animals in their dreamscapes. Hearing her views, at that moment I didn't feel very open to interpreting the presence of dream-bears in my life as emotional confabulations designed to enact impersonal and quite typical male psycho-dramatics.

Giving the psychologist's words much thought, however, I tried to grasp what she said; I tried to listen and learn. Maybe it does make good sense to see myself as just another typical male with typical male coping strategies. The way the mind works is certainly magic enough without engaging in unneeded efforts to divorce one's idiosyncratic situation from the larger human continuum. There are people who have never experienced dreams like mine, but whether or not you've been experienced, all of us together should consider the nature of dreaming.

I suspect that for many people the objective existence of magic bears in the world of human history is debatable. I see their point. I don't take issue with it; but it misses another important point. Maybe my magic bears can't be photographed and collared by science. But as far as my heart is concerned, my dreams are real enough to mean something to me.

We could say at minimum that the narrative of bear-dreaming speaks of my participation in something larger than me and my lonely experience in the world. It's interesting to know that we young men worldwide share something enigmatic, powerful—even profound.

Still, I prefer to picture my magic bears as inherently unfathomable spiritual creatures who manifest themselves in many lives, many minds, my mind. They exist beyond history. Beyond science and science-like knowing. My bears won't ever seem real to cautious scholars in the way they seem real to me. Even if my dreams don't seem very real to other people, they are real enough to affect me, real enough to haunt my inward world where I go to sort things out.

In the story I tell of my life, I prefer to imagine that when I confront things that are truly wrong in the world, when I seek to challenge social injustice, when I try to counter some offense against our humanity—like the idea of race—I do not need to succeed. I need only turn my heart to that problem, and the bears will . . . enact their mysterious purposes. They will do what must be done.

I know this is just a story I tell myself. I have no evidence to justify belief in the reality of my bears. And I have no inclination to even convince myself of any particular truth regarding my magic dream-bears. But I do like this story.

೦೦

Things sometimes happen that have the effect of a real event even if it isn't real. When I was eight years old, for example, I saw a cartoon movie about a monkey that fell into a pool of water and unexpectedly found another world on the other side of it. It was a double-feature in January 1963. My family was on the way to Puerto Rico and one evening we stopped in some city at the deep end of the South and I watched these movies with my sister and two brothers.

For most of my life I haven't known the name of either movie. Now I know that the animated movie was *Alakazam the Great*, an Americanized telling of the Chinese classic by Wu Cheng'en, *Journey to the West*. The second movie took me to a different edge of the earth, to Canada where a Canadian Mountie wore a cool uniform and hat and I don't recall what happened.

The Mountie movie was okay, but the monkey-in-the-pool movie drew me in and I fell happily into its magic. I would think about it every few years and over time it finally became a memory like a dream. On our way to Puerto Rico, I'd say, I went into a dream that someone else had, and I just paid a little bit of money to have it too.

Dreams carry us elsewhere, but I don't know where. They take place as if in a city on the other side of a pool of still water. We must sleep every so often and go back to that city inside because dreams are not optional. You can't live without the mystical realities and confabulations of the dream city-state. Some version of yourself visits there and it means something just as real as though you dwelt in that city and the things that happen to you there are things that actually happen.

At least, this is what happened when I dreamed my seven dreams.

In the Seventh Dream

In the spring of 1976 many things seemed to be coming to a close for me. Disenchanted with school and with writing poetry, I had no sense of where my life might go from there. My girlfriend had left me to try her luck in Florida. By that time I had dreamed many dreams about bears, most of them now forgotten. One day at the beginning of June I resolved to go off by myself and camp alone up in the mountains to mull things over and to think about these dreams. Perhaps a moment of solitude would yield something important for me.

The evening before I left for my camping trip, I went to a party at the house of my cousin Bryce Wildcat. He wouldn't tell anyone when he'd been born, but his friends decided to throw a birthday party for him anyway. There I met a woman who had come down from Montana to visit Bryce, and we ended up at her hotel room where we spent the night together. I felt lonely, lonesome for my girlfriend. Passing the night with Bryce's friend only increased my sense of loneliness.

Early the next morning I hitched up the canyon to my brother's house east of Nederland. I'd been staying there for the previous week or so. After eating breakfast, Walter gave me a ride up past Eldora, dropping me off with my equipment. I used to camp in a certain place in the high valley at Arapahoe Pass, and that morning I hiked for a few miles among great drifts of snow everywhere and soon found a place to set up camp.

I had a small tent and I built a fireplace and gathered some wood. A big, gray camp-robber bird appeared. I fed it some of my food. Cereal. After dark, after the fire burned down low, I crawled into my sleeping bag. Lying there, I eventually fell into a fitful sleep under cold stars.

I don't know how much time passed, but I woke up quickly, hearing something in my camp, snuffling about. I lay there completely still in my sleeping bag, listening to the animal as it moved around through the dark. A fairly large creature it seemed; I felt afraid. I could hear it trying to get at my backpack, deep inside a nearby evergreen tree, leaning against the trunk and containing my food.

After a while, the animal left and I got up and rebuilt the fire. I saw that the stones I had gathered in a circle were scattered in disarray. Fearing that the animal would return, I passed an uneasy restless night. As soon as it grew light I packed up my stuff and headed back down the valley. I noticed that the pack frame was bent near the bottom. A strap had been torn loose. Whatever animal had visited me—it was no chipmunk.

Arriving at my brother's house later that morning I felt exhausted. I went right to bed and fell into a deep sleep. I had a dream. I found myself in an unfamiliar city at night, hiding from the police who were searching for me and for others like me.

Toward morning as it began to grow light, I knelt behind some bushes near a road, watching as a police caravan approached. It resembled a train on the road, a series of small, linked cars filled with prisoners. When this "train" pulled up abreast of my hiding place, several policemen with shotguns leaped out and took me prisoner, making me get into one of the cars.

We pulled up in front of a building and two policemen grabbed my arms and hauled me inside through a set of glass doors. I knew something ugly was going to happen to me. I could hear eerie hopeless screams. The building consisted of one huge room, and the police took me down a center aisle. On either side brooded intricate, very complex machines filled with subtle motions, patterns of light.

Pausing briefly, I leaned over for a closer look into the mass of wires, tubes, rods, and lights. Inside, to my horror, I glimpsed a man—his face contorted with pain as the machine tortured him. He opened his mouth as if compelled to scream, but no sound came out. Panic-stricken, I looked up, backing away hastily.

One of the policemen smiled cruelly. He gestured toward an empty machine. I turned to run toward the glass doors, but the two policemen tackled me and began to drag me toward a couch at the center of the machine, surrounded with mysterious wires, bars, and gears. Numb with terror, I prayed: *don't let this happen to me, don't let this happen.* Then, I sensed something coming. The policemen paused and turned to look outside through the glass doors.

Two bear cubs ran upon the grass. I wept as they galloped through the doors, shattering glass in every direction. The policemen let go of me and went for their pistols, but they could not stand against the fury of those two cubs. I felt so shaken, I couldn't walk. The two bears lifted me and gently carried me outside. We sat down together on the grass.

They seemed eager to play. But restraining themselves, one spoke to me: *don't be afraid. we know you are not a brave man. do you remember last night—the bears wanted to give you something but you were too afraid. we can give you nothing; but since we love you, we will always be here to help you and protect you. there is no need to fear.* They were so tender that I began to weep again. The two cubs turned to go. One of them looked back: *remember*, it said, *remember us.* Then I awoke. I was weeping still, but I also felt a deep sense of joy.

The Moon-Castle Dreams

Ever since I dreamed what I call my "seven dreams," I have continued to dream about bears. Over the years as I explored my way into the dim corridors between sleeping and waking, a bear would unexpectedly appear and wander through the dreamscape. These are typically very placid dreams. These visitors are merely checking up on me, reminding me of their presence in my life.

Their growling happens far off, like a hidden stream in a distant forest.

What are they saying? I can only speculate. Maybe there is no great meaning beyond the way these powerful and mysterious experiences have enriched my life, settling around me an enchanted circle.

I feel grateful. *everyone. I thank you. everyone. . . .*

In the early 1980s sometime prior to November 1982 I began to dream about walking along a quiet stream up a wooded ravine where the magic bears went to meditate. Many bears dwelt in this sylvan place. In each of these dreams I'd be walking up the steep ravine, sometimes along a path and sometimes alongside the stream. I'd begin to encounter bears at some point, but they would generally ignore me, sleeping or sitting nearby, sometimes watching me.

In some dreams I saw many, many bears in the ravine.

I'd go to sleep and find myself walking along and I'd become aware of a nearby bear. I would know suddenly that I was once again in the valley of the bears. Far off at the top of the ravine of the bears, there stood a stone castle with a long stone veranda. This veranda looked out over the silver haze of the ravine to a distant land.

I knew this because I had made it to the top in several dreams. Thinking of a mysterious term I put into a poem I wrote in 1973, I named this mysterious place the Moon-Castle. I dreamed of the path up to the Moon-Castle for twelve or fifteen years and then moved on with the rest of my life.

At the ends of stories we sometimes experience the false impression of having traveled somewhere. Faint landscapes unfold and disappear. Weightless illusions gather and disperse like rain at the end of the road. Pausing between the stories told in these pages, I return to my dream of the mysterious valley where the bears live, and I keep returning there to hear their restless growling and to feel the shallow, buoyant mortality which flows away from us all. The bears call to me and years pass and I find myself among them again.

Far up that valley when I find the courage to follow the path, I know there is a place waiting among the crags like an immense castle. It is a place of living stone with infinite rooms and a long granite verandah which hangs high above the surface of the spinning world.

At every new turn upon the path, at the beginning and end of every story, I am surrounded by bears sleeping in a crevice, bears ambling along the ridge-top, bears standing nearby in the creek. Sometimes two or three come down toward me through the trees and I awaken suddenly.

I feel a very complicated mixture of emotions in these dreams, like they have too much detail. I don't always know if I'm focusing on the right aspect. Do I really grasp how the world works? It is a struggle to decide what to preserve, how to proceed with what I know or what I think I know, to find the secret truths behind the veils of our lives.

The Seeker

I hid from Ralph. He would stroll around the house, around the massive stone fireplace that squatted in the center of our complicated lives. He'd look for me. He seemed very logical and systematic in his searching. I saw how he peered into all the places he thought likely for me to be found at that point in my life. If I could not be found, he'd cry out.

In Colorado Jerri Hof and I rented our final house together and there our experiments in partnership came to an end. At the edge of an ancient mountain forest we dwelt. This vast pine forest drifted away into the mist behind our house. We sometimes wandered down through the leisurely evergreen valleys that fell slowly toward the plains below, far off. Our lives floated above the surface of earth, a restless green cloud always in the midst of changing shape, breathing, alive. There in the mountains I wrote a book of poems and lyric narratives. I watched as Ralph went to & fro at my feet in the mountains and I thought of what to write next.

Jerri had wanted Ralph. A yellow and white kitten. She brought him into our lives in 1976 in Missouri. And she loved him with all her heart and so did I. Together the three of us dwelt in a bustling city at the southern edge of the ancient receding Missouri forest. This was our family during the late 1970s.

Ralph came with us to Colorado in 1978. Several years later he returned with Jerri to Missouri, and soon thereafter he disappeared into the early 1980s. Jerri left him with her stepmother's family in Holts Summit and he ran away. In the summer of 1982 she told me this—the last time I ever talked to her. I asked her what had happened to Ralph.

He might well have still been living when Jerri sat across from me and told me his fate, what she knew of it. Perhaps alive in Missouri through the 1980s. . . . Suddenly I picture Ralph leaving Jerri's stepmother's house, setting forth into the future. I imagine his journey across the dangerous highway. I picture him roaming in my mother's forest in Holts Summit. Maybe he's looking for me. Maybe he even glimpsed me every so often at different points in my life. Visiting Holts Summit, I always walked down the forest road and he could have observed me from the hidden thickets, the cedar densities.

Whatever happened, when it was morning in America Ralph wandered off into the remnants of forest that echoed in Callaway County. In the hilly country north of the Missouri River he wandered. Ralph maybe roamed for a long time there in the greenery of central Missouri, living his years and his final days in the distant northern reaches of the ancient ebbing forest where he had been born.

Curious one day, I ask my mother whether she'd ever seen any stray cats in her forest. No. Her memory isn't as detailed as she would like. Unexpectedly she offers this surviving detail: "I did see a bear once. I pulled up in the carport and sat there reading something and looked up and there was a bear ambling nearby."

Chronology has slipped its mortal coil; she can't exactly recall when this momentous event happened. Maybe, she guesses, about the middle of her years in the wilds of Holts Summit, circa mid-1980s. She recollects no stray yellow/white cats, but a bear did appear there in the late morning of America.

☙

And all the others before Ralph.

Through the haze of my childhood recollections, a cat always stood nearby in my world. Four of them came and went. I like that part of my childhood—many friendly moments among my memories.

And when I was a young boy in late 1966, we got a long-haired orange kitten that wore a slightly darker orange mask. That first day we gave him the name "Raccoon," but within a half-hour or so my father shorted this to "Coon."

Born in the summer in Holts Summit, Missouri, Coon traveled with us to North Dakota, Puerto Rico, and back to the middle of Missouri. He passed in & out of our tales, wandering in & out of those journeys. When I entered the origin stories of my youth . . . when I became a young man... when I became a hippie.

A child of the sixties, Coon dwelt among us in our forest during the epic summer of love when I first read Tolkien's *Lord of the Rings*. And at the end of 1967, when I first listened to the Rolling Stones' *Their Satanic Majesties Request*, Coon couldn't help but listen, too.

ஐ

In the summer of 1968 while living in North Dakota at Minot Air Force Base, we went on vacation to Yellowstone. Coon rode with us in the car, panting under a cool, wet washrag. Somewhere in the Park we pulled over with the other tourists to observe a bear by the road.

When the bear approached our car, Coon jumped up on the rear seat and hissed at it. Ready to fight and not backing down at all, he stood guard until the bear ambled on to the next car. Everyone was surprised and we commented on Coon's bravery, but he just jumped down into the back seat and licked himself in a satisfied way.

We drove on to the Visitor's Center and pulled into the Conoco station to gas up. When the attendant came up to our car in his dark brown corporate uniform, Coon took a good look at him and fled underneath the front seat. In his wisdom, Coon had realized instantly that the Conoco Man seemed far more dangerous and intimidating than any bear could possibly be.

ஐ

At the end of the 1970s, thinking of what my bear dreams might mean, I decided maybe my cousin Bryce was right. Maybe these dreams had to do with being Indian. Maybe I needed to become an Indian. To be sure, I had never questioned the idea of being Indian. Of course I'd always been an Indian, hadn't I? That's how we did race in those days.

But in hindsight it's more complex than that, knowing what I know now about race. Because through most of my childhood and youth, racial Indianhood didn't sink in very deep. I rode the surface of it through the 1960s and 1970s. Approaching the 1980s, it seemed a good time to get into the deeper mysteries of racial identity. To do this, I turned to the study of Pawnee history.

Dreams Like Mine

Long ago my Pawnee ancestors dwelt in earthlodge cities upon the ancient plains in the Land of the Three Rivers and they dreamed of animals. And I sometimes think they had dreams like mine.

What did they make of their dreams? What did it mean to them when bears entered their dreams? A missionary named Samuel Allis lived among the Skidi Pawnees in 1836 and he was told of how they dreamed of bears: "The bear is a great medicine with them, they say the bear is Te war roks te, they sometimes dream of having a battle with them and it makes them brave warriors, they will not get killed in battle, many such superstitions I could mention which are numerous."

Big Eagle, Allis's host, must have been involved in the Skidi Bear Society. This organization held ceremonial dances and the members were viewed as effective and powerful doctors. They could cure illness and wounds and they were successful in war. Women sometimes participated, but most members of the Bear Society were men.

After removal to Oklahoma, the bear societies of each of the Pawnee bands continued to exist as separate groups, but a steady decline in population brought the members together over time, and it became common to find persons of several bands participating in the ceremonies of each society. The primary ritual activity was a dance held during the summer season. But this ceremony drew slowly to a halt.

A Skidi man named Harry Coons wrote about a Bear Dance held by one of the bear societies during the summer of 1889 in Oklahoma. In his letter he mentions how the ceremonial bear-robe wearer, Ralph Weeks, "nearly roasted" from the heat of wearing it on that exceedingly hot summer day long ago.

The Skidi scholar, James R. Murie, published a 1914 description of Pawnee societies in which he wrote about the Skidi Bear Society. It is likely that a Pawnee bear claw necklace now held at the Denver Art Museum was communally owned as a ceremonial object by the Kitkahahki Bear Society during the 1860s. Murie described such regalia in the care of the Skidi Bear Society, who owned four necklaces and other objects. He also wrote a detailed description of Bear Society ceremonialism in 1910. According to his account, the Pitahawirata Bear Society had become defunct with the death of Bear Chief about 1900, but in 1910 it was revitalized after a woman named Yellow Corn Woman had a dream in which Bear Chief called upon the people to hold the ceremony again.

In his final work, *Ceremonies of the Pawnee*, Murie prepared a fascinating narrative told by a South Band man named Eagle Chief about two special bear songs. Eagle Chief told of a man who had learned the mysteries of a den of grizzly bears, learning how the moon "gave its power to Mother Cedar Tree." There were special songs that could be used to heal sick Bear Society members. These were "sung when the moon is very bright in the night . . . for the moon comes with the night, and night comes with many strange spirits that touch people and make them well."

☯

My Pawnee ancestors treated dreams as a special source of teaching. Bears and other creatures could communicate spiritual knowledge and ritual instruction through dreams.

In one Skidi story published in 1906 by George Dorsey and James R. Murie ("The Bear Medicine and Ceremony") a girl is born with the spirit of a bear that had been killed by her father. In adulthood after the death of her son, she is taken into a bear den and given certain gifts and knowledge. Thereafter the bears communicate with her through her dreams, and during the night she grunts like a bear.

This woman became a respected member of the Skidi Bear Society. But she passed on her bear teachings to a Chaui Pawnee man whose descendants held an annual dance each summer.

Many stories like this convey the idea that dreams have quite a lot of interesting things to say about the human condition and are not limited to purely individualistic psychodrama. The human condition is complicated, mysterious. Dreams add something ineffable to this complexity.

☯

For certain dreams at least, in the Pawnee world dreams can be studied not simply for what they say about the dreamer, but for what the universe is saying to the dreamer. Perhaps in the end, my heart urges me to believe that the universe does dream and Fred Alan Wolf's *The Dreaming Universe* speaks a truth that goes beyond the intellectual mind and sends a strange spirit to heal our sleeping hearts.

I like the idea of sifting dreams for insights into personality. The art of psychology and the cultural interpretation of dream symbolism have useful things to say to me about what it means to be human. But we also need storytelling to help us make sense of ourselves. I am drawn to the telling of stories that wrestle with the ambiguities of human experience because the makings of humanity come from both unconscious physical processes and from the artifactual sayings and traditions that enliven mindfulness.

Shaping our notions about dreams, we necessarily draw upon whatever exists around us—a lattice of community and communal knowledge. And encountering the enigma of dreaming, to make sense of it we may choose to deploy many modes of being human, an intricate collage of personhood.

In a matrix informed by Pawnee ideology, dreams of bears have therapeutic power. The forms taken by this mystical healing are determined not by the intentions of the dreamer, but by the invisible sources of life that throng the twilight whispering of the universe. I sense echoes of animals that no one else could ever hope to see, and as these creatures slip into oblivion, I hope for well-being in the world. And I think of how, long ago, my ancestors had dreams like mine.

In an Enchanted Garden

I feel glad to tell this tale, for it is an account of a somewhat mysterious friendship, and telling it, I get to visit a memory of warmth that seems almost magical. But this curious tale deserves remembrance here because it helps me to make sense of the dreams I began to dream long ago in my youth, my bear dreams.

Once upon a time, when I first met my life-companion, Linda Ross, she had charge of a little band of four cats. Jesse governed the realm, a big black cat who went by many names. Rose served as president of Jesse's fan club. She was a tiny thing made mostly of fur. A lonely stray, Mama came to the family pregnant and slightly addled; a quiet daydreamer. The final member of Jesse's posse was Jaxon, a black and white cat born in the late spring of 1979.

In the middle of 1986 Linda and her feline friends opened their family circle and I moved in with them. I soon learned that a special quality emanated from Jaxon. In some mysterious way his warm, wise aura lit our hearts and brightened our home-life. Good years followed under the happy influence of that glow. In our tales of those years, our family world felt to us like a magic circle.

☯

A strange thing happened among us in the summer of 1992. My brother Walter gave me some old Pawnee ceremonial corn that had been carefully preserved by a Kansas seed bank, and I turned it over to Linda. I helped her plant it in mid-May under the chill twilight of the morning star. This speckled corn grew beautifully in her garden. Green leaves sprouted from the small mounds, and we watched as Jaxon made this ceremonial corn garden his new special place, napping all summer under the growing plants.

When we picked the corn in early September and shucked some of the ears to dry the kernels, Jaxon seemed very impatient about it. Spreading the corn on the drying rack, we observed how he eagerly took charge of it. Dense white kernels imprinted with tiny blue bird shapes. Uttering little intent cries, Jaxon would reach in and scoop out a few of these kernels and eat them with great relish.

Looking on in wonder, we decided it had something to do with how he had fallen seriously ill by that time. Taking his troubles in stride, he endured his suffering. But each day brought more precious moments and he wasn't ready to let go. It seemed to us that the Pawnee corn somehow helped him, somehow eased his suffering.

Accepting, generous with love, a little shy, Jaxon reminded me of a long-lost friend I had during the early 1970s. Dennis Smith seemed to bear a mystical and quite profound inner glow that felt like peace to all who knew him. At once young and old he was. A mystery. Jaxon wielded that same inexplicable wizardry.

Hanging out in my office with me at night, Jaxon curled up in my chair behind me in a snug blue cave I made by draping my dark blue robe over the chair-arms.

He slept. I studied history. I wrote poems. A stir at my back. A blind paw. Like someone swimming under moonlight.

Jaxon very much loved wandering in the deep summer nights. Taking a break from my nightly jottings, I'd step outside to smoke a cigarette and he would appear at my feet. A far-off train often whistled like a weird beast hooting under the stars.

That summer of 1992 was Jaxon's final summer with us, when he became our little wizard of the flowering corn.

In October Linda let me take some of Jaxon's speckled corn to Oklahoma and the Morgan family used it in their Kitkahahki Ceremonial Dance. I gave my cousin Helen Norris a basket filled with beautiful ears of Jaxon's corn, thinking that wherever this corn ended up, it would surely kindle a flitting glow in people's lives. There would be moments of peace. Kindness would be done. They would murmur softly, *Let us give thanks for this Pawnee corn and for the wonderful ways of our ancestors.*

In those days, working with my brother Walter, I became known among the Pawnees as a tribal historian. And it wasn't very easy for us to do what had to be done.

But I was lucky; Linda's companionship and Jaxon's friendship encircled the things I did then. They stood nearby as I conducted the research and did the writing that filled my days and nights. They made me feel like I might be doing something special, something worthy of their love.

Did I see that then? I don't know. Whatever I saw in those days, I feel fortunate when I look back now. All those memories feel marvelously epic, as if I somehow found myself in a tale in which my part was modest enough—mundane even—yet those days seem fraught with glyphic meanings that can never be precisely deciphered.

When Jaxon died, we wrapped him in my dark blue robe and it wasn't easy to say goodbye. We buried him in his favorite spot in his enchanted corn garden.

The little wizard wanders at night under the moon. He knows what makes the hidden world work, its secrets, chrome mysteries. His reserved alchemical emotional elixir teaches us things that magically transform our lives into something quite amiable, a clasping of inwardly shining things.

The little wizard curls up behind me. He sleeps as I write. Many strange things I write in the midst of his dreams. I feel glad. For the little wizard awakens our circle; his wizardry understands us.

Everyone smiles. Everyone feels glad.

I Escape from Egypt

In many far-flung cities across the land I came to know James Riding In, a scholar of Pawnee history. At the end of the 1980s and during the early 1990s our paths crossed a number of times. I always felt glad to see him.

I learned of his work from my cousin Bryce Wildcat. Bryce worked at the National Indian Law Library in Boulder, Colorado, and one time James applied there for a job. Bryce knew I'd be interested in the writing sample that James sent with his application, a well-researched disquisition on the final years of the Pawnees in Nebraska.

Later in the 1980s when I began to work with my brother Walter on repatriation issues at the Native American Rights Fund, I mentioned James to him, and about the time I began to get paid as a consultant, I talked Walter into getting James onboard. James proved immediately very helpful. He accompanied us in 1989 to Washington DC as a member of a Pawnee delegation. Suzan Harjo helped to set up a meeting with Smithsonian officials, and James knew things no one else knew. The story he told moved us all, but it wasn't easy to hear.

☯

I spent a week in July 1993 with James Riding In conducting research at the Field Museum of Natural History in Chicago. The Field Museum had extended an invitation to the Pawnee Nation to send a delegation to examine their Pawnee collections, and the Pawnees decided to send James and me. The Field Museum paid for our travel and accommodations.

The first night after our arrival we checked into the hotel and walked over to find the museum. As we approached the museum, one of my cinematic dreams came surging into my mind. Some months before, I'd had a dream about working at the Field Museum among the Egyptian collections.

In the dream I found myself scrambling to escape from the building. I clambered among several huge Egyptian statues in a dark exhibit hall. It wasn't easy to climb the highest section of wall, but I did it. I finally emerged onto the roof of the museum. Looking out into the dream... a bright night lit the arboreal cityscape beyond. This exciting dream stayed with me after I awoke.

While walking with James down the street in Chicago that July evening, this strange dream came back to me suddenly. As we neared the building, a colossal edifice to human culture, we saw that two huge banners had been hung from the roof of the museum. Each of these banners depicted a dancing bear. I felt stunned.

Telling James about my bear dreams, I thought it very significant that these banners with bears should greet us. They seemed to celebrate our arrival. Making a short video of our visit for the Pawnee Nation, we opened the film with a scene of the two bears dancing at the entrance of the museum.

☯

I was in Chicago working to implement a federal law called the Native American Graves Protection and Repatriation Act. Under NAGPRA, Indian tribes—as racially identified sovereignties—are empowered to repatriate human remains and certain classes of items from museums, and the law acts as a compelling affirmation of the status of Indian nations in the American political system.

In the United States Indian tribes are viewed as sovereigns comparable to the US and other nations. But this is only part of the story. The relationship between the US and "Indian" nations arose as a formal matter at the same time that the ideology of race achieved formalized institutionalization in social practice, academic thought, and political discourse.

With the ideas of race in hand, Americans had no intention of treating "Indian" nations as true sovereigns. Within a few decades of the birth of the nation, its legal philosophers had devised an alternate political category for these "Indian" nations. Classed as "domestic dependent nations," these governments assumed a subaltern status in the American system as "Indian tribes" subject to race-based "federal Indian law." Unlike states, which had constitutionally defined voices in the American system, racial Indian sovereigns have never had a formal voice in the American democracy, being instead subject to the dictates of unilateral federal plenary power.

Among adherents to racial Indianhood, NAGPRA has fostered change in the exercise of social power based on race. Meeting the NAGPRA racial definition for "Indian tribe," sovereign "domestic dependent nations" have exercised real authority and have made much use of the law. This situation provides a clear instance of how race has proven useful as a means to gather and wield power and moral authority for adherents to racial Indianhood.

With NAGPRA in hand, many adherents to racial Indianhood feel greatly heartened, and the philosophers of racial Indianhood uniformly believe that race is a good thing. The legacies of white racial injustice can be defeated. And enactment of racial Indianhood really can act to free Indians from white racism, just as the master narrative of racial Indianhood has always promised. For many Indians, listening to the discourse of Indian racial identity in which oppressive white people pose an almost insurmountable obstacle to Indian political and cultural liberation, this is good news.

To be sure, it could well be that this and other forms of racial empowerment will prove potent enough for Indians to achieve whatever they wish to achieve. But here is a more predictable outcome for NAGPRA: racial Indians will enthusiastically utilize the law to willingly bind themselves to the production of American racialism—the same racialism that situates "Indian" tribes in an undemocratic political arrangement within the American political system. By encouraging Indians to bond more fervently as Indians, NAGPRA will further codify race into the mainstream of the racial Indian sovereignty movement, ironically thrusting that movement ever deeper in the embrace of oppressive American racialism.

In the years since my involvement with NAGPRA, I have come to suspect that being free of race will prove a necessary prerequisite for the eventual production of a truly successful sovereign independence movement for present-day "Indian" nations. Racial Indians almost always say they value their sovereignty. To truly liberate Indian nations from their subaltern role in the American political system, what if this must be done by rejecting race?

To my knowledge, no Indian political critic has yet recognized that the challenge to race posed by science and academic scholarship represents a golden opportunity for adherents to racial Indianhood. Choosing the dignity of rejecting a false characterization of humankind, racial Indians have a new opportunity to truly liberate themselves from the tyrannical legacies of race in America.

Oppressed by an ideology formulated in Europe and implemented by adherents to racial whiteness, Indians can now truly dream of independence. Freeing our world from race, today's racial Indians can tomorrow reject their racial status. They can take aim at retrieving their former status as independent non-racial sovereigns by exploiting a new opportunity to dream of whatever they wish to happen next in the story.

In the Eighth Dream

Waking one morning in 1996, I passed out of an intense dream in which Jaxon came to visit me and Linda. After Jaxon's death in early 1993, Jesse did his best to serve as our remaining feline companion. Now in this dream, Jaxon felt excited to see me again, galloping happily around our green lawn.

As I watched him I thought I noticed something odd. Jaxon kept turning into a small black and white bear—an energetic bear cub running in and out of focus. And once when he paused next to me he reached out a paw and I felt his claws press sharply against my leg. At that moment a thousand glittering thoughts rushed through my dreaming mind.

I stood there listening for many years it seemed. I heard a somehow familiar voice: *We just wanted to be with you for a time . . . we have been glad these years to spend this time here, and we will always be with you.*

I realized then that Jaxon and Jesse were the two bear cubs in my dream of long ago. They were the cubs in my "seventh" bear dream. Marveling, I thought: What a privilege to have known them in this world and to have had their companionship.

A wonderful, warm feeling. Watching Jaxon a moment longer, I gradually drifted awake . . . returning as if through a glowing valley into this world. A place we share with marvelous creatures.

Hearing the mysterious tales told by our dreams, we understand that dreams represent a form of storytelling that is only partly rational. Dreams get constituted from logical and illogical components, quantifiable and unquantifiable sequences, predictable and unpredictable outcomes. Dreams have plenty of plausible precision, but they are also rich with sidelong meanings that elude precise analysis.

This perpendicular explanation of dreams is not logical. But it is necessary.

In the story I tell about the weirdness of dreamlife, I have a fateful invisible essence that coexists with the measurable quantities that comprise my visible human form. It is an immeasurable quantity. Like a soul, a spirit, an inner transcendent consciousness. We all have this aspect of selfhood. All living things.

When we dream we invoke this essence. And this dream-self dwells in a realm somewhere at an angle to the one we know in our waking lives. And when it enters our reality, it finds itself in a place that doesn't make sense, just as we encounter confusing mysteries. In this ineffable place of boundaries our logical minds and our mysterious essences must discover a new logic. Our essences and our minds must enact a different kind of drama, talking soul to soul.

What gets expressed often sounds strange when we listen from this side of our dreams. For it is inherently a way of talking that transcends time and space. When we talk over there on that side of things, perpendicular to the logical rationality that we know here, clarity isn't always very clear. Clarity is too simple.

We must guess at what happened. We must tell this story in a way that sounds both wise and foolish. This storytelling isn't logical, but it is necessary.

When I think of this utter complexity, I feel glad.

Jesse's final years with us were quiet years. An elderly cat in his late teens, his hearing dimmed, and for several years he often thought Linda and I might be sneaking up on him. He had this thing he would say on such occasions, a sharp little cry that meant *What the fuck!?*

Going about his business in a world full of steadily receding sounds, old Jesse had no idea how we had learned the cat-skill of creeping up on him so quietly. We had spent years trotting around the house like a couple of wheezing noisy elephants. Suddenly here we were padding about like two giant cats.

One day in October 1996 I wrote down what I came to call my "eighth bear dream." I felt the need to record the magic of it, how Jaxon and Jesse became the two bear cubs of my seventh bear dream long ago in 1976. A week later Jesse died. His work was done. Linda and I buried him in Jaxon's enchanted garden.

Pondering my eighth dream, I learned something interesting. From one angle, I knew these two cats had a special place in my emotional life. From another angle, when my soul sought meaning in its secret world, it found Jaxon and Jesse wandering beyond the boundary between waking and sleeping, and they appeared at my side as two bear cubs.

☙

In 1996 I was just beginning to consider the news about race. As an Indian I had never doubted the idea of being Indian. So the news troubled me. I slowly came to the conclusion that race does an injustice in our social world. It deceives people. It warps the nature of our humanity. It corrupts our storytelling.

In the story I tell of my life, whether or not I succeed in my doings, I need only turn my heart to the problems that must be faced. And my two companions will stand at my feet—a place of boundaries.

And the magic bears will . . . they will enact their mysterious purposes. They will do what must be done.

This is the secret story I tell myself.

And on the fifteenth anniversary of Jaxon's death, Linda had her own bear dream. She dreamed of a bear cub, a black cub. Kittykittykitty, we kept saying to it in her dream. For it wasn't just a bear—it was Jesse!

In our tranquil circle... our clasping of inwardly shining things... we are glad. Jesse and the little wizard wander at night under the moon, bent on inexplicable errands, perpendicular to the places we know.

The little wizard curls up behind me as I write. Many strange things I will write.

And Jesse visits Linda. And knowing her heart, he watches over our little realm. And he knows what makes the hidden world work, its secrets, chrome mysteries. And he will teach us things that will magically transform every part of our lives into something amiable and very pleasant.

And everyone smiles. And everyone feels glad.

5

Slowly Unraveling

Circuitous Tomorrows, Refinished

I often visit a very special place where the people aren't completely real. Oh sure, every person there has a name and a face, and each one comes with plenty of the things that go into the making of a bona fide lifetime. But this particular place only exists online as a virtual reality, and it is a place where the people choose to do race.

It is known as the Closet Chicken Coop. When I was an Indian and believed in race, I could never have foreseen the future that would come upon me as a Closet Chicken. And in my tales of the Coop, when I speak of race I mean to say that even though race is composed of unfinished ambiguities, it is nevertheless relentlessly convinced of its certainties, and it has an aura of inevitability. If everyone stays loyal to the traditions of race, a racially finished future will inevitably spring up from an equally finished racial past.

Race wants us to picture tomorrow and the day after tomorrow without ever bothering to suspect that we ought to have a choice about the kind of past we could have in the future. But when I was an Indian I didn't mind the idea that race had it all planned out for me. I'd be an Indian in the future and I'd stand there in my tomorrows and I'd look back at my yesterdays and I'd see an Indian. I wouldn't mind. Not one bit. In fact, I'd like it very much, thank you.

While considering this fate one day, I stood silent at the door of the Coop. Observing the Chickens doing racial Indianhood in such a collegial way, as they have always done it, I thought I knew how they felt about it. They do what they do for the sake of the future. Historians want us to believe that the present is shaped by the past, but the present is shaped by the future at least as much as by the past.

With this truth in mind, to truly understand my storytelling about the Coop and what I did among Chickenry once upon a time, I must take a rather circuitous route back to a previous millennium before there was a Coop, and I must talk about a particular era in my life when I did race but I knew it had some problems and I gradually realized that I didn't want to do it forever. In those days, rejecting the future that race had carefully planned for me, it seemed impossible to want a present with a different future, a future with an unknowable past. I had to figure out how to accept an unfinished present inspired by the ambiguities of an unfinished future.

To tell this strange story, I must touch on what is known among racial Indians as "repatriation." Eventually I'll move on to say several very unusual things about racism and racial whiteness, and if the future finds you reading to the end of this story, you'll find yourself meandering back for another visit to the Coop.

But first, before setting forth in time, a little about the mythos of the Coop. . . .

☯

The Closet Chickens sprang up in 2001 as an informal online collective of archaeologists who mostly identify as adherents to racial Indianhood. Unified by the mission of providing a counter-narrative to American archaeological storytelling that developed with little input from racial Indians and their communities, the Closet Chicken paradigm is one of racial social justice. Toward this end, they don't do archaeology; the Chickens do race-based "indigenous" archaeology.

Surveying the discipline of archaeology from the postcolonial perspective of the Coop, the view is informed by race and the politics of racial polarity. In the story promoted throughout Chickendom, the mighty edifices of insensitive white archaeo-colonialism tower over the oppressed villagers of Indian archaeo-indigenism. To fulfill their quest to racially "decolonize" the doing of archaeology in Indian country, the Closet Chickens seek to wrestle with various race-based social dilemmas on behalf of Indian people, and it is believed that the lives of these racially identified Indian people will gradually improve as these struggles gradually succeed.

This quest seems almost impossible. But racial indigenism is nothing if not heroic. Progress may well materialize if indigenists stay dedicated to expanding the moral authority of racial indigeneity, and if indigenists diligently police the monumental inertia of white archaeology, and if indigenists thwart the frequently misguided and sometimes malignant intentions of racial whites. These are some of the basic communal ingredients for the production of indigenous archaeology.

In expanding certain well-established epistemological horizons, in combating racial injustice and its legacies, and in making archaeology more inclusive as a profession, the Chickens deserve a voice in twenty-first century archaeology. But when the intellectual agenda involves the promotion and empowerment of race and racial loyalties, challenges seem appropriate.

Entering the Coop at the dawn of its origin story, I challenged the racialist components of this indigenous archaeology. I hinted at various problems presented by reliance on racialism. I called for dialogue on how race functions in the making of indigenous archaeology. I reminded the Chickens that race was born in Europe, not America. And I explained that racial Indianhood arose from the study of skulls in the principalities of

Germany, not from the mystical visionaries of the Great Plains. And I sometimes wondered whether race inherently undermines the sovereignty of racially self-identified Indian nations. And every so often I said that race fundamentally warps the tales we tell about ourselves.

I guess it seemed polite to set forth my thoughts on race and racial Indianhood first with colleagues for whom these ideological systems were intimate matters of personal identity. Hoping that the Closet Chickens would prove interested and supportive colleagues, I discussed many such things as I stood inside the door of the Coop at the beginning of another new century, another new millennium.

The Coop became a place for me to experiment with devising an effective analytical perspective on academic racialism. Coming to describe myself as "anti-race" and "non-racial," I really meant to say that I had a commitment to not do race rather than a commitment to force others to stop their racialism. It came to seem more important to develop an introspective form of anti-race discourse than to proselytize new converts into promoting anti-race activism. In fact, it seems rude to aim at convincing people to reject race. People deserve choices, not arm-twisting.

But what the academy does is another matter. The academy should refrain from promoting race and from suppressing race, and academicians must help us all by cultivating a position of neutrality and by seeking to develop an accurate critique of racialism—one which actively engages the anthropological rejection of race as a theory of human physical diversity. We must grasp what it means to redefine race as a cultural practice rather than as a biological truth.

And since the academy helped to give us race, the academy ought to feel an obligation to help give us a real choice about race. We deserve a non-racial alternative. In the future I wish for, the academy will help us make our own decisions about whether to do race. And in fact, for many people already. . . .

But now we have jumped somewhat far ahead in the story, jumping past the beginning and the middle of it. This particular tale really begins with the end of my days as an Indian. It has a dreamlike texture to it, like something that didn't really happen, and yet it did happen.

It happened long ago. . . .

The Obsidian Mirror

When I was an Indian writer and an Indian scholar I wrote about what it meant to be an Indian in a white world. The last paper I wrote while still a full-fledged Indian was called "Reflections on Repatriation." Assembling it in 1996–1997, I had just begun to encounter the news about race and I hadn't yet decided to give it up.

It's no wonder that I had a strong sense of racial identity. Encouraged to fulfill my designated role as an Indian in racial America, I had earned a master's degree in history with an emphasis on "ancient Indian history." Now I had a job working to implement the Native American Graves Protection and Repatriation Act (NAGPRA), a law that epitomized what had come to be called, during the twentieth century, "federal Indian law." As an adherent to racial Indianhood, I became a willing cog in an entrenched social machine that intended to forever churn out the cultural thingamajigs and widgets of race.

Back then I was a racial idealist—racialism seemed both unavoidable and worthwhile. I wanted the production of race and the manufacturing of racial Indianhood to mean something positive, something good in the world. And I had a sense of certainty about what the enactment of race signified.

But maybe I never quite succeeded in figuring out exactly what kind of important thing we were all doing with the thingamajigs and widgets of race. Performing race in daily life is more of a journey than a destination, and since the journey is what gives meaning to racialism, you don't necessarily have to spend much time thinking about where everyone might be going.

Nevertheless, it all seemed perfectly obvious at the time. I didn't mind bonding with other people via a shared commitment to race because I pictured myself as a promoter of social justice. I didn't give much thought to where race planned to take us all—I had plenty of things to say even if I didn't know where we might be going.

With such things in the back of my mind, I wrote "Reflections on Repatriation: Images of Academic America in the Mirror of NAGPRA." I got the idea of the mirror from an archaeologist named Dorothy Lippert. I met Dorothy in the spring of 1996 at the annual meeting of the Society for American Archaeology in New Orleans. This proved to be one of the conferences that ultimately helped to give rise to what was already becoming known as "indigenous archaeology." Dorothy soon became an enthusiastic proponent of this race-based intellectual movement. In her 1996 paper, "In Front of the Mirror: Native Americans and Academic Archaeology," she set forth the early foundations of her thinking.

As a racialist, I felt sympathetic to Dorothy's agenda in those days. I particularly liked the way she encouraged archaeologists and Native Americans to look for common ground. Seeking a poetic lens to focus her thoughts, Dorothy referred to an ancient obsidian mirror from Central America and she pictured how she and the original owner had each peered into it across time, seeing "similar" images. She ended the paper with a pan-humanist appeal to the reflected image of our common humanity.

I have the impression that in the years after 1996 Dorothy moved beyond appealing to we-are-one idealism in favor of appealing to the bonding power of racial Indianhood. Glimpsing Dorothy and her many colleagues every so often upon the Red Road here in the twenty-first century, I sense that they know exactly where they are going with race, with the idealism that empowers Red Pride racial bonding.

If it all works out the way they intend, someday the continued advancement of race as a social project in America will give racial American Indians a better world—race will help Indians fulfill their aspirations. As a means of gathering social power, racial Indianhood has indeed achieved some notable victories. NAGPRA is certainly one. The hope is that there will be new successes if Indians stay true to racial Indianhood and if everyone else stays true to race. Toward this end, the twenty-first century factories of racialism are even now gearing up to turn out many excellent thingamajigs and shiny widgets for loyal adherents to racial Indianhood.

This is the essence of the master narrative of racial Indianhood.

No matter that racism is the typical noxious byproduct of the zealous doing of race. No matter that this predictable outcome of race gets no introspective contemplation from practitioners of racial Indianhood. Can the manufacturers of Red Pride Indian identity really avoid polluting the social environment with racism?

For Indians at the end of the twentieth century, racial Indianhood stood for opposition to entrenched white racism and its oppressive legacies. Moving to oppose white racism, Indians gave everyone the impression that they would never stoop to the making of red racism. The implication was that racist practices are done by racialists who are unworthy in some manner, such as racial whites, who proved prone to the making of things like eugenics and Jim Crow segregation. In contrast, Indians would prove worthy, untainted—the noble epitome of multicultural racial humanity.

The problem is that these assumptions are inconsistent with the reality of racial practice. History tries to tell us that racism is the typical noxious byproduct of the zealous doing of race. So it seems useful to suspect that even a cursory examination of racial Indianhood will reveal that socially empowered Red Pride racialism is just as racist as socially empowered White Pride racialism. Forever honing critical skills on the analysis of white racism, Indian intellectuals have little interest in critiquing racism in the practices of racial Indianhood. In the absence of anything like critical inquiry into red racism, no one really knows where the fervors of racial Indianhood will take us.

One destination, at least, seems clear enough. Proponents of Red Pride racialism openly intend to strengthen the idea that loyalty to one's race should serve as a legitimate defining social mechanism. And in the archetypal vision of race-based social justice, adherents to racial identity systems plan to keep the machinery of our social world forever engaged in producing the ideological artifacts of racial fidelity. All will stay true to race; all will be faithful to the idea of racial group identity; all will preferentially bond with members of their own race.

Anyway, hearing Dorothy Lippert's paper at that conference in 1996, I decided that I liked her obsidian mirror and the pan-humanist images it reflected. I guess I'm one of those we-are-one idealists. So when she turned away to talk to another Indian for a moment, I took her mirror to use in my next paper. Following the logic of we-are-one idealism, I eventually found my way onto the non-racial path that I tread today.

I went on tour in 1997 with Dorothy's mirror and my new paper. Phil Deloria arranged for me to read the first draft of the paper in early January 1997 at the plenary session of the annual meeting of the American Historical Association in New York City. In September I took a longer version to Wyoming—Wyoming Archaeology Awareness Month had come to the state, and a distinguished archaeologist named Larry Zimmerman and I had been invited to give papers as the "Keynote Lecture." Several years later the archaeologists in Wyoming very kindly published both of our papers in *The Wyoming Archaeologist*.

That was a nice thing to do, though I haven't ever been very comfortable with the way they edited my paper. Among other things, they turned James Riding In into James Riding. I like the name Riding In. It's a beautiful Pawnee name and it has always bothered me that the archaeo-editors in Wyoming took out that In. Because without that In, James has nowhere to ride, he's just Riding. Someday, I said to myself, I'll repair that irritating editing error.

Finally looking at "Reflections on Repatriation" in 2005, I decided that even though I might not agree with the way they edit things in Wyoming, I saw that the paper did need some sprucing up. I pondered whether to rewrite the whole thing and disempower the thingamajigs and widgets of race, but instead I opted to preserve the racial essentialism of my thinking in 1997.

I had once been a willing cog in the implacable racial machinery of our world. Peering at my abandoned pro-race assumptions in the mirror of my present-day non-racial anti-race perspective, "Reflections on Repatriation" memorializes the power that race wields in shaping and distorting our communal storytelling, like this:

Reflections on Repatriation, 1997

A dynamic landscape of relations exists between Native Americans and the American academic community, and as the final days of the twentieth century approach, it is important for us to contemplate the legacy of relationships that we will pass along to our successors. The topic of repatriation has played a prominent role in shaping this legacy in recent years, particularly for archaeologists. Repatriation involves a deep set of issues rooted in historical circumstances that are often obscured by the debate over its immediate implications for the academic world. And these circumstances are complex.

In the disciplines of history and anthropology, scholars throughout the twentieth century scrambled to record what they viewed as an ever-vanishing Native America. Despite this perspective, Indians have sustained a continuing presence in American scholarship. Poised upon the vast interface of history and anthropology, ethnohistorians at mid-century made academic inquiry into Native America a multidisciplinary endeavor, and in the decades that followed, Indian history became established as a viable enclave in academic history. Indians have always held a prominent role in American anthropology as informants and occasionally as scholars, but the one-way mirror of American anthropology became a two-way window during the 1970s as a result of Vine Deloria Jr.'s scathing critique of the profession. Archaeology also fell under the spotlight of this scrutiny, and archaeologists trained to investigate extinct cultures found themselves, increasingly, excavating the heritage of living—not dead—societies.

The civil rights movement in the United States created an atmosphere of social change for African Americans, and it inspired Indians to address a variety of human rights issues. They spoke out against the codified practice of treating Indian burials and human remains as archaeological resources subject to excavation, scientific study, and permanent curation in museums. State laws carefully regulated the treatment of non-Indian cemeteries, and these laws accommodated the rights and sensibilities of the non-Indian American public, but archaeologists routinely excavated Indian skeletons and funerary objects for permanent service to science with little or no regard for the rights and sensibilities of interested Native communities.

જ⊗

Many archaeologists and most physical anthropologists focused very quickly on the religious perspectives which figured so prominently and consistently in the objections of Indian leaders, and the issue was framed as one of science versus religion. This focus encouraged many archaeologists and physical anthropologists to overlook or minimize the important issues of cultural oppression and the exclusion of Indians from social control over funerary settings. Since the academic community rejects the idea that religious protests should dictate the content of scientific research, many scholars relied upon the principle of academic freedom to emancipate them from any sense of connection to the historical circumstances under which Indians lost control of ancestral cemeteries. For scholars, the establishment and curation of collections of Indian skeletons could symbolize the exercise of academic freedom, while for Indians such collections signified a continuing history of oppressive dispossession.

Living Indians participated in various realms of scholarship throughout the twentieth century. Persisting in American society, their expanding engagement with academic America has introduced new changes in the disciplines of anthropology and history. In the 1980s, the architects of the New West opened the door for historians to recognize Indians as a continuing presence in the American world. As this recognition gained strength in the field of history, archaeologists of the time also found themselves confronted with Indians advocating the reburial of Native American human remains. Throughout the academic community, Indians were no longer expected to vanish, but scholars had long scrambled to subject disappearing Indians to the scrutiny of science, and now the academics themselves were being scrutinized by living Indians.

જ⊗

Responding to decades of pressure from Native Americans, Congress passed the Native American Graves Protection and Repatriation Act of 1990 (NAGPRA). Under NAGPRA, Native Americans assume a greater administrative presence in the practice of archaeology, and Native communities have greater power to re-establish authority over culturally affiliated human remains, funerary objects, and other items held by American museums and universities. In essence, the law has aided in the continuing process of recognizing and accommodating the active presence of Indians in American society.

While some observers view NAGPRA as an important factor in bringing about a needed adjustment of relations toward greater accountability to living Indians, others have openly resented the loss of unscrutinized authority and unfettered inquiry, and they worry about infringements upon academic freedom. NAGPRA does not incorporate any statutory impediments to academic freedom, but the impact of the law upon the ability of scholars to advance historical knowledge is a matter of great interest—as well as a topic of much debate—throughout the academic community.

Observers in the archaeological community vary in characterizing the impact of NAGPRA on their world. Borrowing an ideological framework from geology, those who see NAGPRA as a logical and necessary development of relations with Indians might be said to have a "uniformitarian" perspective, while "catastrophism" offers a useful paradigm for those scholars most fearful of its impact on science and archaeology. Thus, in a recent issue of the *Society for American Archaeology Bulletin*, Terence Fifield reports favorably on the "truly gratifying spirit of cooperation" between Indians and scientists in dealing under NAGPRA with the discovery of ancient human remains, while G.A. Clark of Arizona State University informs the editor of the *Bulletin* that "NAGPRA is an unmitigated disaster for archaeologists, bioarchaeologists, and other physical anthropologists concerned with the study of human skeletal remains."

In contrast to this spectrum of academic opinions, few Indians are worried about the impact of NAGPRA on scholarly endeavors. Opinions among Native Americans reflect a strong interest in successfully implementing the law as well as open suspicion that it merely serves a firmly entrenched non-Indian system that remains fundamentally opposed to the cultural values of Indian communities. For some Indian leaders, the denunciation of academic scholarship is based, in part, upon a rejection of science, while for others, a critical perspective on the academic world coexists with recognition that important purposes are served by scholarship. In fact, successful implementation of NAGPRA is highly dependent upon access to reliable scholarship.

Few Indian repatriation programs have adequately accommodated the reliance of the law upon the expertise of historians, archaeologists, and other scholars. Though tribal historians are sometimes placed in charge of tribal repatriation programs or are asked to serve as advisors, the title of "tribal historian" is often an honorific which does not come

with any salaried institutional appointment designed to support research projects on tribal history. Some tribal historians are well-versed
in the esoteric details of religious and cultural lifeways, but have little or
no experience with the skills required to investigate provenience information, to study ethnographies for evidence about the historical character
of tribal laws, and to research the cultural affiliations of past societies.
Of the many tribal historians who do have these skills, few have the
personal resources to support research projects in these critical areas,
and Indian tribes typically have limited resources to support research
needed for repatriation claims. It would therefore be the height of cynicism for scholars and their institutions to refuse to work in partnership
with tribes and then to proclaim NAGPRA a failed concept.

With regard to the treatment of human remains, the American academic system has a rather dismal record in attending to the concerns of Native American communities, but non-Indian Americans expect to hold
science accountable for actions which offend public sensibilities. During the late 1780s in New York, for example, when white Americans discovered that medical students were appropriating human remains from
their cemetery, the citizens rioted. As a result of the Anti-Dissection
Riots, science learned to live with limitations on the use of the remains
of white Americans for bona fide research of unquestionable benefit to
living people. The passage of Anatomy Acts at both state and federal
levels ensured that interested researchers would not ignore public sensibilities in their professional conduct.

Meanwhile, Thomas Jefferson, the founding father of American archaeology, helped to create an important and enduring double standard
when he neglected to consult any Indians in conducting his excavation
of an Indian cemetery mound at Monticello. But there were no riots in
Virginia. Over the next two centuries, scholars would faithfully adhere
to this standard. In the Anti-Dissection Riots, doctors throughout New
York City fled for their lives and took refuge in the jails; by contrast, Indians today have been, for the most part, remarkably civil in calling for
change and seeking legislative solutions to the circumstances of scholarly interest in their dead.

It is important for academic institutions to encourage self-review on
this topic, and, more generally, they need to promote an ongoing process of internal inspection of the state of overall relations with Native
American communities. The images we see in the mirror of NAGPRA
may not be flattering to institutions which depend on public goodwill

for support, but goodwill should never be lacking for institutions that are willing to gamble on intellectual integrity over a polished public relations image. Historians such as Robert Bieder, Orlan Svingen, and James Riding In have researched the history of academic interest in Indian human remains, and such research can continue to play a critical role in this self-review process.

In New York, for example, the American Museum of Natural History provides us with an important opportunity to reflect upon the mirror of NAGPRA. The museum recently made the remains of Qisuk, a Greenland Eskimo, available for burial. Kenn Harper has written a compelling account of Qisuk's death a century ago, describing the deception perpetrated upon his young son, Minik. For Minik's benefit, the staff of the American Museum pretended to bury Qisuk, but actually kept his skeleton for science. With the burial of Qisuk in 1993, an important sign of change emerged from the American Museum. Reviewing the broader picture of this museum's accomplishments, we ought to take pride in this museum which has contributed so much to the quality of American life through public education, but this pride should expect accountability, and it should prefer that accurate self-review provide a basis for setting the academic agenda for the future. Under NAGPRA, little chance exists that the story of Qisuk and Minik will be repeated.

In Colorado, the quest to establish and maintain the dominion of the United States affected both living and dead Indians. One hundred years ago, in July 1897, a woman named Mrs. M. E. Crowley visited the State Historical and Natural History Society—the predecessor of the present-day Colorado Historical Society—and made a rather gruesome donation. A tag attached to the object recorded the donation as the "[s]kull of a Ute Woman who was killed on the western slope of Colorado in the year 1885."

Research mandated by NAGPRA tells a tragic story which might never have been told without this law. In June 1885, two Ute families camping near Dolores, Colorado were attacked by local whites in an incident known as the Beaver Creek Massacre, and it is likely that the skull collected by the ghoulish Mrs. Crowley came from one of the victims of this unprovoked slaughter. For the founding fathers of the Colorado Historical Society, this donation signified a contribution to science. They had a sense of purpose that did not reflect any inclination to form partnerships with Indians; in fact, to the vast majority of white Coloradans of the time, Indian people were simply obstacles to be overcome, dispossessed, and controlled. It was a minor leap from the idea of controlling living Indians for the convenience of white settlers, to the idea of controlling dead Indians for the convenience of science and scholarship.

The Ute skull was examined in 1981 by James Hummert, a doctoral candidate in physical anthropology at the University of Colorado, and he concluded that the skull was that of a "[c]hild about 12 years old." The circumstances of Hummert's research project reveal much about the academic attitudes that ultimately gave rise to the need for NAGPRA. In response to what was termed "[m]inority political activism," CHS funded a study of their human remains in order to underscore the significance of this collection for scholars, and Hummert was hired to conduct this research. The contract was deliberately prepared as an unadvertised project due to fears that it would attract "untoward activist activity."

Hummert wrote in his final report that the collection of human remains held great value in terms of "educational and research potential." Ironically—given the secretive nature of the study—he also offered the hope that skeletal research might someday be appreciated by Indian people. Indeed, his research proved extremely helpful to CHS in preparing reports required by NAGPRA. Nevertheless, as with the story of Minik, the conduct of this study emphasizes the fact that the academic community in the United States has felt free, as a matter of convenience, to actively exclude living Indians.

Opponents of NAGPRA fear that the law may hamper the progress of science, but the law was designed to bring Indians into the picture in order to discourage unrestrained trampling of Indian rights and sensibilities in the name of research. The law was not designed to thwart legitimate scholarship. Too often, NAGPRAphobes seem blissfully unaware of the history of deliberate exclusion of Indians from academic endeavors, and we are given the impression that the choice we face is one of enslavement to the whims of anti-science Indians versus a return to the good old days of conquest anthropology.

Unlike their colleagues in the medical profession, physical anthropologists and archaeologists have had little accountability to the people who are most directly interested in the human remains they collect and study, and so they have been free to pursue unfettered research. The Anatomy Acts did not put an end to the legitimate interest of the medical profession in the study of dead bodies, and we have little reason to believe that NAGPRA will put an end to the need for physical anthropology as an important field of study. More than ever, in fact,

Native American communities need the services of skeletal biologists and physical anthropologists. In my opinion, the ideal Native American repatriation program would involve administrators with expertise on NAGPRA, religious leaders, and tribal historians, as well as professional academic historians, archaeologists, physical anthropologists, and other scholars.

While physical anthropologists as a group choose to indulge an unproductive resentment toward Indian reburial efforts, it will be difficult for them, under such circumstances, to assist tribes when their expertise is essential to clarifying the identity and cultural affiliations of the dead. Physical anthropologists often point out that their knowledge could benefit Indian people, but such words sound hollow when they are not accompanied by efforts at dialogue with Indians, and when they are uttered primarily for the edification of journalists intent on embarrassing proponents of reburial.

Under NAGPRA, Indian communities have a new relationship with academic institutions, and the character of this relationship *can* affect the ability of legitimate researchers to conduct important investigations. Physical anthropologists, for example, have legitimate interests in conducting research that many Indians may find objectionable. As a result of NAGPRA, if any of these interests are threatened, it is because scholars have consistently failed to earn the support of Indians. Thus, science would best be served if scholars have a relationship of mutual respect with Native Americans—a relationship in which the interests of science can be articulated by researchers and endorsed by tribes.

Such relations would also constructively reflect the concern felt by many physical anthropologists that Indian people can benefit from access to meaningful information about long-dead ancestors. It will take time to overcome the powerful legacy of distrust that tends to dominate present-day interactions, but in the long run, skeletal biologists can best serve the future heirs of their profession—which is beginning to include both Indians and non-Indians—by embracing a clear commitment to developing partnerships, rather than lawsuits, with Indian tribes today.

๑๑

The national press has given impressive coverage to the discovery in 1996 of human remains dubbed "Kennewick Man" in the state of Washington. Inspection of the skull revealed the presence of "caucasoid" characteristics, and a radiocarbon test performed on a finger bone indicated that the person died about 8,400 years ago [later tests push back this date to over 9,000 years]. In addition, a projectile point from a time period of about 4,000 to 9,000 years ago was found imbedded in one bone. These circumstances attracted the interest of the Confederated Tribes of the Umatilla Indian Reservation, who filed a claim with the US Army Corps of Engineers for the repatriation of the remains under NAGPRA. As the Corps moved to comply, following NAGPRA guidelines, a group of leading American anthropologists hired lawyers and intervened in the situation, asking a court to postpone the repatriation to allow additional scientific study. This strategy of adversarial confrontation, however, maximizes the opportunity for mutual alienation and minimizes any chance to build meaningful relations with interested Native American communities. One might suppose, therefore, that little common ground exists between these parties.

In a statement authored by a religious leader and issued by the claimant tribes, the hostile tone of several remarks about scientists implies that extreme polarization is also the favored Indian position. It is notable, however, that the Umatilla Reservation hosts a well-established tribal archaeology program that has provided hands-on experience in archaeology for a number of reservation residents. In fact, one graduate of this program, Philip Minthorn, is employed by the Repatriation Office of the National Museum of Natural History—the Smithsonian museum which employs several of the scholars who intervened to halt the repatriation. In essence, the parties have not successfully made effective use of an excellent opportunity to build mutual goodwill by developing a cooperative program of some sort.

In the initial opinion of the Army Corps of Engineers, the claimant tribes did not need to demonstrate any cultural affiliation in order to obtain custody of the Kennewick human remains under NAGPRA, but the situation has changed as a result of more careful evaluation of map boundaries, and it is now important for the claimant tribes to show a cultural affiliation. Any demonstration of cultural affiliation must consider and accommodate anthropological evidence, and since the position paper of the claimant tribes asserts an affiliation on the basis of oral traditions, this assertion must also be considered.

Most scholars doubt that oral traditions can contribute legitimate evidence pertaining to historical settings of such antiquity, but the contribution of oral traditions to scholarship on ancient Native America presents an unanswered mystery of increasing interest to researchers. In the case of Kennewick Man, however, we are left to wonder whether or not it is possible to connect the anthropological evidence with evidence from Indian oral traditions. It should be a matter of interest, for example, that at least some archaeological evidence has been interpreted to suggest great time depth for cultural continuity in the region. The comparison of oral traditions and archaeological information might yield unexpected congruities—but this possibility is dependent upon a commitment to dialogue based on mutual respect.

༄

Direct dialogue will create solutions to important challenges faced by Indians and archaeologists who wish to work together. Some Indians and archaeologists will not wish to work together; the paradigm of science versus religion—embraced by both groups—will continue to act as a polarizing force. Considering Kennewick Man, an annoyed Victor Mair portrayed Native Americans in a page of a 1997 issue of the *Anthropology Newsletter* as "[doing] their utmost to prevent scientific investigations on ancient human remains[.]" Summarizing his research on "caucasoid" human remains in western China, Mair holds forth the Chinese government as a model of accommodation to science, in contrast to the situation in the United States. Mair seemingly would prefer that American Indians have no say in what happens with their dead. Nevertheless, he advocates standards for archaeologists and physical anthropologists that would find great favor among many Indians.

Mair spent two years negotiating with the Chinese government for permission to conduct his investigations, and, according to his account, the local ethnic population which claims descent from the subjects of his study also supports his work. Mair lauds this support as the inherent right of science, but he spent two years negotiating the terms of his research with a government controlled by an ethnic group with no significant biological connection to the caucasoid subjects of his study, and he is properly cognizant of the interests of one group which claims actual descent from the population in question.

It is difficult to understand why Mair takes a partnership approach in China and then articulates another standard for the United States— a standard of professional conduct that would reject any need for a meaningful dialogue with Indians. If ancient caucasoid human remains in China can be controlled by a non-caucasoid Chinese government, and if Mair can acknowledge the existence of a complex web of interests at work in China, then the picture in the United States can be expected to display no less complexity. Using Mair's example, it would be to the benefit of scholarship in the US for American researchers to conduct sustained negotiations with interested parties, such as Indian tribes, and scholars should seek to accommodate applicable national interests—as expressed in laws like NAGPRA—before proceeding with research plans. It is reasonable to expect scholars to expend some effort toward the development of mutually beneficial relationships with Indian tribes. If American archaeologists are willing to embrace cooperative partnership as a desirable relationship with interested parties in China, then such standards should also apply closer to home in the United States.

໑໑

Viewing academic America in the mirror of NAGPRA, a diverse collage of images appears. Universities, historical societies, and museums must acknowledge the images that their own experts see in that mirror, whether the images are admirable or embarrassing, and scholars should expect their peers to adhere to a standard of professional conduct in which Indian tribes and Native Americans have real access to accurate data and scholarly knowledge. It is reasonable to expect scholars to devote some energy toward earning the trust and support of Indian tribes in order to pursue research goals that will create useful data, lead to reliable interpretations, and generate interesting ideas. Cooperation with Indian tribes does not necessarily mean that academic scholarship must forgo the opportunity to contribute to the complex, ongoing heritage of human intellectual endeavors. It can be an extremely fruitful investment of energy in which both groups participate as partners in a dialogue.

Indians also need to acknowledge that NAGPRA will only be as worthwhile as the scholarship that implements it. It provides a real opportunity to subject the American academic community to scrutiny for ongoing insensitivity toward Indians, and scholars must endure the criticism of a newly empowered constituency toward whom they have historically felt little accountability. Native Americans have wielded minimal direct influence within the institutions of academic America, but NAGPRA has changed the rules.

Tracing some of the circumstances which led to this change, we glimpse a world of deeply entrenched racist agendas, an American double standard over the graves of the dead, a scientific community freed by the processes of conquest to indulge unfettered interests, a vast legacy of images in time. Even so, among the many ideas we can bequeath to our heirs in the next millennium, in my view the idea of "partnership" offers an essential concept for shaping a shared future for our human past.

Reflections on Racism

In 1996–1997, writing "Reflections on Repatriation," I didn't think of myself as a racist. In the story I tell of myself, I stood up in those days for racial Indianhood against white injustice. I stood up for the principles of social justice, for fairness, for mutual respect, for Indian empowerment, and for multicultural partnership among the races. But standing up for the making of race, for the committed enactment of racial Indianhood, was I also standing up for racism?

"Reflections on Repatriation" seems a useful place to assess this question. Looking at the paper in October 2009, it reminded me of how I was a racialist long ago. I believed in doing race. Everyone did it and so did I.

Was I also a racist?

ᖇᖇ

My conception of race today includes two components: *racialism* and *racism*. It's important to distinguish and define these components as an aid in applying critical analysis to how race actually works in our world.

Racialism is the cultural idea that humankind is composed of racial groups that are biologically distinguishable according to physical attributes—attributes that are arbitrary in selection, definition, and application. Racialism is purely faith-based because it believes without scientific evidence that the concept of race offers a valid depiction of human biological diversity.

But racialism is not scientific because it visualizes racial groups as definable islands with settled boundaries. In reality, science provides no justification for the existence of such boundaries due to the gradient nature of genetic traits as they are actually found throughout humankind.

Racism can be defined as the preferential ranking of racial groups. Racism flows directly out of racialism, but it explicitly or implicitly sets forth a defined ordering of racial groups according to some standard of preference.

According to these definitions, if one believes in race and accepts the groupings of race, one is a *racialist*. If one takes those racial groups and employs forms of ranking to order the groups in some preferred fashion, one is a *racist*. Racism is exerted in American society as an exercise of power of some kind—power of variable intensity that is designed to discriminate against or in favor of a targeted racial group.

These are very general definitions that we can apply to our everyday world and our behavior in it. But there is more to consider. In accordance with my definitions, *racism* must be recognized as an activity that is pervasive throughout American society, not as something done by a shrinking group in our midst.

As a society, when we make the charge of racism, this is usually intended as a negative moral judgment. But in my usage, racism can actually have a more complicated moral and ethical setting. This is because the practices of racism can be usefully ordered along a commonly employed moral spectrum. At one end is what I term *unilateral racism* and at the other end we find *conjoint racism*.

In *unilateral racism* an individual or a group has made some kind of preferential determination that is applied without the input or consent of other affected groups. This happens, for example, when "white" realtors engage in red-lining—a practice designed to exclude "blacks" from certain "white" residential neighborhoods. This is not a common racist activity today, but it was once a fact of American life in many places.

In *conjoint racism*, multiple racial groups have gotten together and have jointly agreed to assert some form of preferential racial ranking. This is presently the most common kind of racism in American society today, and it is usually done with little or no negative moral objection.

All forms of racist practice, however, necessarily enshrine and perpetuate the precepts of racialism regardless of what kind of moral judgment we attach. Racism always involves race-based discrimination of some kind, and unilateral racism and conjoint racism differ primarily in the moral conclusions we draw about them.

In the twentieth century American racialists developed an effective critique of unilateral racism as a problem in American society. And this has been the dominant theme of the American civil rights movement for many decades, resulting in significant changes in the character of race in the United States. This change over time tells us that the fundamental ideological materials of race flow from historical process, and that race consists of enormously mutable concepts and outcomes. As my definitions reveal, the civil rights fight against racism has not been comprehensive, but it has certainly enjoyed significant success in its more limited targeting of unilateral racism.

Another important question must be asked. Can conjoint racism be a good thing for society? If the answer is yes, then a viable argument can be made for the doing of race as a social project. In American society here at the beginning of the twenty-first century, the typical answer is that conjoint racism is unremarkable; it is usually socially benign; and it can sometimes indeed be a good thing. This is a common assumption.

In my view, attacking unilateral racism while promoting racialism is problematic because it is an inherently self-defeating enterprise. Since racism emerges from the dehumanization of racialism, unilateral racism will never go away so long as the sustaining roots of racialism are free to nurture it.

But if conjoint racism is a good thing—if multicultural racialism is good for humankind—then perhaps modest amounts of the lingering byproduct of unilateral racism can be tolerated. But only if conjoint racism really is a "good thing."

Race is a nebulous theory in practice, but definitions of racialism and racism are of dubious social value if they do not encourage and support useful analytical insights. To apply my definitions of these concepts in a practical way, we can go back for a second look at the opening sections in my 1997 paper, "Reflections on Repatriation."

I begin this paper with a statement that sets up my intention to discuss one form of race (racial Indianhood) in the context of one form of academic culture (archaeology): "A dynamic landscape of relations exists between Native Americans and the American academic community. . . ." This doesn't sound racist; most people would pass over this statement without any special notice.

But if we peer beneath the benign surface . . . how do the assumptions that empower this statement compare with my definition of racism?

First, I manufacture race by assuming that people can really be sorted out into distinct racial groups. Using the term "Native American," I treat racial Indianhood as a biological identity limited to people with an Indian genetic heritage. There may well be plenty of people who engage in the same practices and beliefs as "real Indians," but in the absence of the proper kind of "blood," race won't permit them to ever be "Indian." In short, I don't see race as a cultural construction.

Second, to assess the potential racist content (as I have defined racism) we should next look for some form of race-based preferential ranking. I think it can be found in my usage—I believe that racism exists as the embedded logic of the very making of race itself.

By asserting that particular individuals can be selected in biological terms and cleanly distinguished from the milling herd of humankind, I am indeed performing an inevitable "preferential ranking." *You are an Indian; you are welcome to stand over here with the other Indians! You are not an Indian; get back into the herd!* This ranks people by creating a special pseudo-biological class of individuals holding membership in a racially segregated group. Indians. Thus, the very use of race terminology is fundamentally racist because it involves an unavoidable preferential sorting process.

My analysis here suggests that race cannot be performed without racism; racism is the underlying vitalizing essence that enlivens race. So what kind of racism does this reveal? What manner of racist was I back in 1997?

As a matter of common protocol in the 1990s, describing people in terms of race was a conjoint project—a project that everyone openly engaged in without fear of social censure. My deployment of "Native American" in the first sentence of "Reflections on Repatriation" is therefore a perfect example of conjoint racism. I was a racist, but I didn't ever worry that I'd be held accountable in a disapproving way by anyone in America. It was something we all did openly. Together.

It is arguable that we should reserve the use of the term "racism" only for unilateral forms of racist behavior—behavior forged as a weapon by members of one group in order to harm and oppress another group. This approach would preserve the term's ability to express a distinctive negative moral judgment, which is important in combating unilateral racism. But both unilateral and conjoint racism spring from the same systematic ranking procedure. The same process used to forge the unilateral weaponry of racism is also deployed to forge the basic notions of racial groupings themselves.

Utilizing the processes of racial identity necessarily means implementing some assertive degree of racial allegiance. As a minimal result, the intended outcome of self-identifying in racial terms is to validate race-based categories. The degree of assertive racial allegiance is often mild enough to qualify as a form of conjoint racism—that is, it would not attract any special attention as a violation of tolerated social practice. But it would nevertheless qualify as "racism" because it assumes bona fide membership in a racially defined pseudobiological class which is preferentially exclusive.

In short, announcements of racial identity are always intended to sort people out into artificial and preferentially selective groupings, and as a matter of typical practice, reliance on racial identity is fundamentally racist because it cannot avoid systematic hierarchical rankings. So when race gets overtly expressed, we should be thinking critically about the degree to which racism is also a covert ingredient of the practice.

This truth of racial practice deserves acknowledgment, conscious awareness. In terms of public morality, both unilateral racism and conjoint racism should be seen as racist; and more importantly, both forms of racism deserve moral scrutiny as dehumanizing assaults on the nature of our humanity. Doesn't this outcome deserve some form of moral judgment?

Racialists often bond with one another by denouncing as racist some unfortunate bumbling doer of race who says or does something deemed offensive. My definition of racism intentionally reframes the issue as one of analytical precision. We non-racial anti-race advocates must preserve the critical utility of my definition of racism because if we are to ever make possible a non-racial cultural option in America, we will need useful analytical insights. Seeing race as fundamentally racist, and understanding that the doing of race is inherently inescapably pervasively racist, we must reject the inclination to bond via the production of racialism.

ഭ

At the opening of "Reflection on Repatriation," presenting a historical synopsis of "the disciplines of history and anthropology," I engage in race-talk that could be easily retranslated into the way I talk about race today. I comment, for example, on the fact that racial Indians didn't vanish during the twentieth century: "Despite this perspective [the Vanishing Indian stereotype], Indians have sustained a continuing presence in American scholarship."

As a practitioner of conjoint racism, here I clearly intend to rely on the bioracial use of race terminology. But this statement could be easily revised to conform to a non-racial analytical perspective: "Despite this perspective, adherents to racial Indianhood have sustained a continuing presence in American scholarship." Substituting "adherents to racial Indianhood" in place of "Indians" decisively shifts my intended meaning away from passive acceptance of racial pseudobiology and toward a conscious emphasis on the true character of racial identity as a cultural belief system.

A useful tactic of what I term "non-racial anti-race discourse" is to delete or minimize reliance on the everyday usage of racial taxonomy and terminology. But this tactic isn't appropriate when the discourse is intended to comment on the doings of actual or arguable adherents to racial identity. Given the fact that racial terms reflect cultural ideology and not biological truths, if we agree to passively accept traditional usage of race terminology, we necessarily abandon the treatment of race as a product of culture.

ഭ

In my 1997 paper I wrote that "[twentieth century] archaeologists routinely excavated Indian skeletons and funerary objects for permanent service to science. . . ." The matter seemed clear enough at the time I wrote those words. As I saw it then, archaeologists routinely dug up Indian graves during the twentieth century.

Were I to write this statement today, it would go like this: "[twentieth century] archaeologists routinely excavated the skeletons and funerary objects of persons deemed to be racial 'Indians' for permanent service to science. . . ." There is a qualitative difference in deploying the terms of race in a way that conforms to traditional racist practice, as opposed to crafting, from a non-racial perspective, a useful analysis of the practices of racist racialism.

To say—as everyone put it in those days—that "archaeologists routinely excavated Indian skeletons" is to raise another important issue. Archaeologists of the twentieth century routinely dug up an awful lot of my Pawnee ancestors, but not all of those people were "Indian." It is accurate enough to say that archaeologists who routinely dug up my ancient ancestors had the unscientific notion that they were digging up Indians, but a non-racial historical analysis of this activity has the responsibility of making judgments about whether this characterization is indeed accurate.

It is impossible to dig up an "Indian" if the remains in question are not arguably those of a practitioner of the identity system of racial Indianhood. Racial identity is a cultural system, not a biological reality, and we know that modern forms of racial identity evolved into common practice during the late eighteenth century. For this reason, it is no more possible to dig up the skeleton of an "Indian" who lived at circa 1000 CE than it is to dig up a "Democrat" of circa 1000 CE. It remains possible, however, for an archaeologist to dig up one of Roger Echo-Hawk's ancestors who lived circa 1000 CE. Reconfiguring the way we talk about racial identity is an important project of the non-racial anti-race agenda.

Toward this end, archaeologists of the twentieth century who saw themselves as engaged in the socially useful project of digging up Roger Echo-Hawk's ancient "Indian" ancestors must be understood as practitioners of an entrenched belief in race. They didn't ever see themselves as digging up pre-racial ancestors of adherents to racial Indianhood. They just dug up Indians. Archaeology, I suggest, must learn to do things differently in the twenty-first century.

In 1996 when I started writing "Reflections on Repatriation," I still thought of myself as an Indian, even though I was actually just an adherent to racial Indianhood. By the time the paper appeared in print in 1999, I had a more complicated picture of myself. I had begun to reject race, but I didn't know how to do it.

Holding that publication in my hand one day in 1999, I felt a momentary pang of dismay. This paper did race and I didn't wish to do race. How would I ever not-do race? Maybe I'd forever find myself holding publications just like this one.

During the late 1990s I worked to implement the Native American Graves Protection and Repatriation Act at two museums in Denver. At first I saw myself as an Indian and I expected everyone to see me that way and that's how all my colleagues saw me. I was an Indian. This sense of orientation changed very slowly in me. But the end of that particular day eventually came for me. As part of my effort to detach myself from the constraining social realities of race, I decided I had to leave my job in Denver and I made a variety of decisions about how I would disengage from and engage with the racial world.

It has been important to me to stand free of race in order to seek some new standpoint from which to critique race. As a personal matter, I reject race as an insult to the nature of humanity. But dealing with the established communal culture of race in America is a matter that is necessarily fraught with ambiguities that call for subtle complexity in our thinking. Race deserves to die, but what should be the fate of the social creations of race?

In this context, my thoughts have often turned to NAGPRA. Considering the fiercely loyal commitment of racial Indians to the traditional structures of race, it seems realistic to picture Indians as a group staying true to race for both the near future and the foreseeable future.

As the future of race moves toward inevitable sunset, rather than participate in rethinking race, the culture of Indian political activism seems poised to keep heroically breathing life into racial Indianhood. Knowing that historical anti-Indian American patriotic nationalism has often sought to limit and terminate racial Indian sovereignties, the philosophers of Indian law have necessarily aimed at institutionalizing and even extending the racial work of race-based federal Indian law and statutes like NAGPRA.

What will happen to federal Indian law if America ever sets its sights on truly creating a race-free cultural option for Americans? No one knows the answer. But the answer will not be simple.

I have the impression that the future will happen, and Indian leaders will very slowly begin to sense that national support for the continued making of racial Indianhood has faded into a gently gathering lack of momentum, an absence of enthusiasm for doing race, a vastly stolid inertia. Perhaps most non-racial Americans will mainly want to get on with their race-free lives and will be content to let Indians do whatever they wish with the remnants of race. But given the continuing interest on the part of a few Americans in terminating racial Indian sovereignty, benign disinterest about the changing social meanings of race doesn't seem likely.

I wish I knew what the future holds for the fate of federal Indian law, for laws like NAGPRA. Of all the things I know and might know and don't know, this is one thing that I surely do know. To play a meaningful role in shaping the coming future of race, Indian law philosophers must act now rather than later.

☙☙

Today I find it useful and easy to describe myself as a former Indian, a former adherent to racial Indianhood. But when I was an Indian, I would have resented being told that I wasn't really an Indian. It would have felt disturbing had someone said to me, "You know, Roger, I've always thought that adherents to racial Indianhood are pretty fascinating!"

In fact it happened every so often that some new acquaintance did say to me, "You know, Roger, I've always thought Indians are pretty fascinating!" It invariably made me feel . . . a twinge of creepiness. And I could never figure this out because it seemed like an innocent way to start a polite conversation.

Adherents to racial Indianhood sometimes report a disconcerting feeling when a white person deploys a romanticized stereotype of racial Indianhood. You feel vaguely unsettled, like you've just heard something racist. You know it would be rude to call "racist" the nice person who just complimented you by admiring your race. And you yourself admire your race, so how can it be racist when you feel that way too? This moment feels awkward in a puzzling way.

Now I think I have an answer. This feeling occurs when such racially essentializing comments come from well-meaning white people—that is, from people identified as racially white.

And so we come to a hidden truth that many of us began to sense by the 1990s. And this is a very important hidden truth which is already shaping the future of race.

A growing majority of "white people" aren't actually white.

To understand this assertion, we must first accept the idea of treating race as a cultural concept rather than as something in our physical selves. Shearing race of its phony biological underpinnings, we must necessarily reject the idea of racial identities as collections of behaviors and ideas produced by biologically discrete human populations. Instead, the quality of racialness comes down strictly to behavioral patterns. With this definition in hand, we must conclude that racial identity consists of engaging in specific cultural behaviors that facilitate bonding processes centered on embracing and validating pseudobiological stereotypes.

This subtle distinction is greatly significant. It means that in order to accurately characterize racial practice as "racial," it is no longer enough to describe the cultural behaviors of people deemed to fit a racial group. To do so, in fact, is to continue to embrace the central tenets of racialism. Rejecting the dubious bio-logic of racialism, we must necessarily redefine racial identity in a way that is not fraught with the discredited assumptions of fake biology.

This can only be done by looking for an underlying intention to socially enact the discredited presumptions of race. In other words, adherents to racial identity adhere to their preferred identities by purposefully selecting cultural behaviors designed to promote a shared sense of bioracial heritage, a sense of pseudobiological community.

Thus, to have a racial identity, one must deliberately choose to enact preferential bonding processes which involve the social production of specific racial stereotypes. In short, if "white people" do not actively participate in the production of racial whiteness, then they are no longer "white."

It means something quite consequential that significant numbers of alleged white people have fundamentally rejected the notion of bonding through the vilified cultural practices of racial whiteness. If this is accurate, it means they have successfully abandoned the pleasures of race.

ଚଚ

As I see it, in the history of race during the late twentieth century, it gradually became a social expectation for adherents to racial whiteness to live life without racial bonding. "White" people who have lived by this code must be forced into doing race by other more diligent practitioners of race.

Somehow this point should be obvious, but it isn't—as if it happened when the rest of us weren't looking.

I'd guess that it started perhaps as early as the 1940s when white Americans began to see themselves as the saviors of America. They saved America from the grasp of Nazi Germany—*from the grasp of a white master-race cultural agenda*. To tell this heroic story properly, it became important to reduce reliance on white racial identity and to emphasize instead a patriotic affirmation of non-racial pan-human values. For this reason, by the 1960s a large number of white Americans sat up one day and realized they felt ready to grant racial blacks full civil rights.

Most of them didn't exactly know why they felt this way. Believing, as they did, in an empty version of race . . . even so, race still had plenty of muscle in America. And race refused to permit these "white" people to fully realize the truth. They went on through life calling themselves white, but it was a lie because they didn't do race when racialists weren't looking at them.

Plenty of white people during the 1960s and 1970s liked being white and wanted to keep on with being white. But as they drifted toward the 1980s these active practitioners of racial whiteness slowly found themselves practicing their racialism with an ever-shrinking pool of fellow whites—a population cohort that became a decidedly modest clique of fringe-types by the end of the 1980s.

A minor resurgence of fringe-element white pride happened with the coming of skinheads, Christian Identity, and the militia movement. But in 2008 a racial black man got elected president, not a skinhead Nazi Christian wearing fatigues. Racial white people didn't prevail. And they knew early on what had failed—huge numbers of race-traitor former whites had abandoned the de-hallowed tenets of white pride.

So by the time I began reburying my "Indian" ancestors, ever-growing numbers of "white" Americans had spent their lives bonding through everything but racial whiteness. The traditional list of socially available white pride cultural customs had begun to seriously evaporate, and many of these so-called "white" people did nothing in their daily lives to affirm and practice their lapsed allegiance to racial whiteness.

To be sure, it's arguable that many former whites of that time found incidental occasions to engage their lingering racial whiteness. But I'd guess that for them a racial identity option, at best, had come to serve as an insignificant mode of identity. And this class wielded little, if any, cultural authority since they identified closely with former whites who more diligently promoted the idealism of rejecting white racial bonding, and all such "white" people felt indistinguishably intolerant of the cultural agenda of white pride whites.

In general, as the end of the twentieth century approached, ever-increasing numbers of "white" people found they didn't much care about race. This didn't dawn on everyone one day in a big flash of light over the earth. It very slowly crept up on the world, and no one really noticed.

Hearing these fake white people congratulate me for my racial identity, it didn't feel very sincere. I knew perfectly well what it looked like to enact racial Indianness, to serve as a correspondent on Indian affairs for a literary newspaper, to work for an Indian law firm, to help my race improve its circumstances. Yes, I knew what it looked like to do race and to live it with my heart.

So I must have had the awful feeling somewhere inside that these weren't really white people. I guess I got the vague impression that they might be humoring me just because they knew that I valued the doing of race. This was an unconscious nagging feeling. It lurked beneath the surface of awareness—my muscular racialism wouldn't let this realization burst out openly into my thoughts.

This meant that when a putative white person who didn't really care about doing race stood there telling me what a fine thing it was for me to be an Indian, it felt vaguely creepy. In hindsight I guess I had trouble respecting people who acted like racialists were people to admire when they themselves did so little of race in their own lives.

๏๏

The non-racial anti-race analytical perspective set forth here offers a practical explanation of what race means in our world. In terms of racial whiteness in particular, I suspect that every former white person out there very much needs to hear this message because it will help them to explain their lives.

It also explains the present-day trend toward embracing what is being called a "postracial" outlook. Former white people find themselves bored with the doing of race because they themselves don't do it and they get along just fine without race. Being committed to racial social justice, as many of them are, they are willing enough to embrace the idea of being white when asked to do so—they want to get along with people who value the doing of race.

But it's a tiresome business. They have learned that we can get along in life without relying on race to help us find our way. Daily life in mainstream America doesn't need to revolve around the storytelling of race.

I feel doubtful that people who rely on race for some kind of meaningful affirmation—like race-believing Indians—will feel very pleased to hear this news. When Indians look around at the world, race wants them to see real Indians and real white people and other such traditional racial things.

Having traditionalized the culture of race for generations, and seeing race as a bulwark against the end of time immemorial, many Indians will not want race to go away. Many Indians will not want the rest of us to get along without race. If they can manage it, these committed practitioners of racial Indianhood will seek to make race a permanent communal requirement for the social contract in America, an immutable clause in the American way of life.

All will do race. All must believe. And if we are pure in our belief and if we are loyal to this purity, together we will gladly endure the suffering of race.

Indians count on the power of conjoint racism to make their case on behalf of racialism. The doing of race today requires both conjoint racism and unilateral racism to succeed as a social project. Examples of unilateral racism must be constantly propped up in American life as validation for the practice of conjoint racism because as long as there is an arguable need for conjoint racism to counter the evils of unilateral racism, Americans will keep on doing race as a matter of social justice. This is a strategy that seems doomed. Race is doomed because it has already died among ever-expanding numbers of white people. Race does not tell them who they really are, and they know it. And if they don't yet know it, they deserve to know that race isn't necessary. Race is optional. It is possible to be non-racial.

Whether race sits at the center of your life and identity, or whether race resides somewhere at the edges of your selfhood, the fate of racial whiteness tells us that we must begin to rethink some fundamental social truths in the world. But this will not be easy.

For those of us who give ourselves permission to change, we must do our best to get along with people who will never change. We must respect the choices others make for themselves, and we must expect them to respect the choices we make for ourselves.

I think this seems like a good place to begin.

The Heroic Hatchlings

In October 2009 I posted the original version of the above material on my website. The next morning, visiting the online Closet Chicken Coop, I found a disappointing email from one of the Chickens. This email had to do with the birthing of new Chickens.

Established in 2001, the communal protocols of the Coop have never been formally chiseled in stone, but a set of customary practices gradually evolved around the process of adding new members. These rules guided the group as it grew from a handful of founders to over seventy members by the end of 2009. During this period, as the flock expanded, it moved forward with its own agenda—the agenda of a racially driven indigenous archaeology.

Selective in admitting new colleagues to their ranks, the Chickens became a racially divisible group with the membership comprised primarily of self-identified adherents to racial Indianhood, together with a handful of self-identified white archaeologists. New eggs got incubated and hatched as racial Indian archaeology practitioners became identified by a member of the Coop and had their names submitted for membership. If no objection ensued, their names got added to the roster.

On the October morning in question, one of the Chickens had written a note to clarify the group's consensus on membership nomination procedures. The note explained that "non-Native" nominees had to receive endorsement from a minimum of two "Native" members of the Coop. Furthermore, there had been talk about restricting "non-Native" members from nominating additional "non-Natives."

I hadn't heard of these special measures. The Coop assembles annually at the meetings of the Society for American Archaeology, and I presume that discussions held in the course of these gatherings had led to this rule-making. These measures seemed designed to purposefully restrict the ability of "non-Natives" to participate in the finding and feathering of new members.

I felt sad to read this email. Then it dawned on me that as a former Indian I wasn't "Native," so I had to be "non-Native." Now I felt angry. But with the Coop chock-full of Chickens bent on fighting racism—white racism—I thought for sure that someone would object, so I checked my email through the day. After six or seven new emails materialized, I saw that the Coop had swiftly moved on to its usual business of bonding through the traditions of racial Indianhood.

Back to feeling saddened, disappointed. Did the Coop enjoy doing race so much that it would embrace racial discrimination rather than fight it? I heard in my mind the voice of one of my mentors, a man who had told me the year before about how he'd gone to jail in Virginia forty-three times during the early 1960s, fighting institutionalized racial discrimination. Had all those battles been waged in order to make it possible for racial Indians to indulge in discriminatory practices based on race? I decided I had to speak out. I sat down that afternoon and fumed, composing a first draft.

I started off with a harshly scathing "Kloset Khicken Koopsters" and continued on with a few sarcastic ideas for advancing the new racist agenda of the Coop. I suggested that our non-Native Chickens "ought to have the decency to sit in the back of the Coop," and that perhaps we needed to post a Sergeant-At-Arms at the Coop's door, Munsell color chart in hand, to send incoming "Chickens Without Color" around to the side-entrance "to make sure they don't get unpleasantly mixed-in with any Chickens of Color." I ended up with the observation that "I am quite beside myself to see that things are finally unfolding in the Coop in such a way as to give everyone an equal opportunity to see what kind of superior uplifting moral fiber Natives are made of, as opposed to the rather dubious fibrous substances non-Natives are made of."

Finishing, I felt better. But I . . . I decided to let my feelings simmer a bit—it didn't seem at all fair to compare the Chickens to the KKK. The members of the Coop may be many things as individuals and as a group, but they just aren't the kind of people who would brutally victimize and terrorize their ideological enemies. And perhaps my passive-aggressive sarcasm would discourage some of them from speaking up. I saved this email as a draft. The day passed; late evening came and went.

In the deepening night I decided my angry sarcasm seemed too melodramatic. More importantly, my bitter response over-inflated the significance of these racially biased membership guidelines. Perhaps this was negligibly mild conjoint racism at work, an inconsequential moment in the Coop's noteworthy quest for social justice. But still nursing some disappointment, I began to prepare a more reasoned critique of the Coop's membership policy.

By the next morning, with no commentary in my inbox, it had begun to seem that the Coop's race-based policy on membership rights had come across to the Closet Chicken mainstream as unremarkable. All the Chickens milled about, feathers unruffled, complacent.

Finalizing my commentary, I stood up to challenge Chickendom's pro-race idealism and sent this note winging into the Coop's inbox:

Critiquing the Coop's racialist consensus, I have looked at things from a non-racial position. This necessarily means that I am a "non-Native" since I am not a racial Native, so I am now disturbed to learn of my second-class status in the Coop. It greatly saddens me to think that I could not help to nominate a so-called "non-Native," and that the Coop is even going so far as to seriously consider totally ignoring me if I were to propose, on my own, a fellow "non-Native" for membership in this group. In fact, given the sense that these racially segregationist gatekeeping measures seem to have already been implemented in the Coop, "saddened" does not come close to capturing the offense I feel. I worked at the Native American Rights Fund and I did consulting work for NARF and I associated with NARFers for years in the course of my life, and I didn't ever see anyone treat the NARF "non-Natives" in such a discriminatory and demeaning fashion.

In this posting on Coop membership policy, the author accurately characterizes the general direction taken by the Coop from the very beginning. The Coop has always preferentially selected its membership on the basis of race, ameliorated by occasional selection of a few carefully vetted "non-Natives." This production of conjoint racism is a common approach to do-

ing social justice in American racialism, but the Coop now seems intent on correcting even this moderate inclusiveness by rounding up and herding its "non-Natives" into their own little reservation. I don't quite understand how racism really can be useful as an appropriate empowering engine for an authentic social justice agenda genuinely aimed at defeating racism.

Whatever individual Closet Chickens may embrace as their individual purposes in the Coop, it is my opinion that Chickendom's shared social agenda is not well served by explicitly engaging in overt racial discrimination. This form of racism ought to be rejected as a basis for defining the Coop's shared group identity. Toward this end, I have always felt that all Closet Chickens deserve the dignity of full and equal enfranchisement as full and equal participants in the doings of the Coop.

A quiet day passed; I found myself alone in a silent Coop. All the Chickens preened themselves in the unknown darkness beyond my little roost.

That evening I sat down to watch a television documentary about the Nazi state archaeology program, the Ahnenerbe project, a nexus of ultra-nationalistic racial ideology and racism. The Ahnenerbe archaeology agenda involved an embarrassing effort to unearth an appropriate "Ancestral Heritage" as a means of shoring up the notion of a Germanic master race and building a world in which all are forever committed to the principle of racial loyalty.

Pondering possible comparisons to the Coop's energetic investment in a race-driven indigenous archaeology, I concluded that some comparisons exist, but tend to be thin. Throughout the historical development of archaeology as an academic enterprise, nationalism and racialism have intersected at many points along the way, but the Nazi outcome stands as an extreme example of the dangers of mixing race and nationalism and scholarship. The Coop is pro-race and favors Indian nationalism and supports the doing of archaeology, but it is difficult to imagine that proponents of indigenous archaeology would ever become willing participants in carving the kind of ugly swathe in archaeological intellectual history made by the Ahnenerbe project.

Even so, sitting there watching the program, I knew I didn't like the idea that indigenous archaeology might in time move toward (rather than further away from) greater intellectual compatibility with the rampant racialism of the odious Nazi program. Following the logic of race, perhaps the Coop needed oppositional criticism to help moderate the temptations of the superpowers of racism. I'd guess that none of the participants of the Ahnenerbe program raised anything like a dissenting voice. If they did have a dissenting critic in their midst, then surely that person's pleas fell upon deaf ears.

Had my plea fallen on deaf ears?

Perhaps it is the measure of a healthy social discourse in an academic discipline for there to be oppositional criticism in the dialogue on controversial topics, and for these conditions to be willingly countenanced, even cultivated. Racism does not like this kind of intellectual environment, I presume. So what did my dissenting objections engender among the Chickens?

The day before I submitted my criticism of the Coop's membership policy, one Chicken had made a mildly crude joke. Another Chicken responded with what sounded like a rebuke, and the jokester immediately apologized.

Standing up the very next day to issue a genuine heartfelt complaint of offense about racism, I wondered what to expect. Did I expect an apology?

Quietly roosting through the days that followed, a few of the Chickens surely paused for a fleeting moment before turning back to... to their continuing efforts to unearth from the depths of racial Indianhood an appropriate ancestral heritage.

☙❧

Pondering what this might signify, I told myself that it's easy to make an honorable apology for a casual joke gone awry. And it might be somewhat less easy for the Closet Chickens to sort out my aggrieved apprehension about the fundamental doing of what the Coop does.

For the Coop does race. All the Chickens gather to do race, to make sure that race gets done upon the earth. And the proud doing of race is what the Coop looks for when it pauses to peer into its collective mirror. And seeing race, they like what they see.

Rebuked by my protestations, it is the rebuke itself that feels awry to some of the Closet Chickens. And some of them might even feel that an apology is due. If this is so, it is because of a heartfelt truth that shapes the experience of race.

You see, in doing race, racialists have all suffered. The doers of race have made one another suffer for doing race. Everyone has suffered and everyone has heroically endured through the long anguish of racialism.

They are heroic, the Closet Chickens. And they intend to pass on their suffering and their heroism to their heirs. Believing that the cost of doing a little racism is a fair price to pay for the honor of this indomitable mission in life, the future will surely reveal their labors and their distress to have been notable, worthwhile, resolute. Their heirs will thank them for passing on intact the heroism of racial Indianhood, for bequeathing the chance for everyone to feel intrepid and to bravely carry on.

Peering today into the days that will come... when the Chickens gather in the far future before their forever unfinished obsidian mirror, all will peer into the mirror to dream of enduring ever more of the long unending years of the anguish of race. For this is the dream of racial Indianhood.

6

The Enchanted Coop

In the Realm of the Bears

In tall mountains among evergreens I stood
above a glittering brook—on the other side
seven or eight people strolled along a trail
downstream under sunlight to a campground
a cheerful flock of Closet Chickens, another
gathering of the Coop, these friends laughing
and nearby, not far, a bear, ambling aimlessly
on my side of the dream I turned to look away
through the trees and meadows and yes I saw
another bear moving faster, purposeful—was it
coming toward me? I slipped into cool water
thinking to swim across to avoid an encounter
but the first bear took notice, paused, watching
I returned to the shore, returned to the meadow
seeing the second bear splashing in the river
clever drops flashing from profound paws
the two creatures intent on each other, they
had little interest in my doings, my notions
I circled around them for the campground
I would warn the Chickens about the bears
I knew they'd all feel grateful, thankful &
& suddenly I saw many bears everywhere
just like so many other times I stood there
in the midst of another assembling of the
bears, I stood alone; and all the Chickens
had left; I realized they already knew, & I
& I guess no one had thought to warn me
& yes I felt alone but I didn't mind, that's
okay because I knew the bears yes I knew
what it was like, like this; I noticed the last
Chickens leaving on another path among
evergreens, so I followed them, and a man
on a bike drew near and I waved him off
bears! & I saw another couple, two people
I didn't know—don't go that way; and I
walked near the river again, glittering waters
flowing forever through beautiful mountains
on the other side strode a man with two dogs
along the distant trail, tiny figures hiking on

toward the bears; I tried to call to him & he
couldn't hear, too far off—somehow I knew
he thought his two dogs would protect him
here in the realm of the bears... maybe so
but they'd be afraid, those dogs; and next
two women followed, two friends trekking
in the mountains in my dreaming and no...
no... I guess they just couldn't hear me

The Magic Children Closet Chickens

The Closet Chickens hatched on the internet during the late spring and
early summer of 2001. In our origin story, race created Chickendom in the
image of race and everyone expected to share a common path.

The Chickens would be Indian archaeologists in a white world.

But having given up race, I didn't share this vision of things. And
suspecting that the Chickens might decide to go on doing race, I wanted
to at least hear some good reasons for doing it.

Still, I felt optimistic that they'd be willing to listen to my questions.
Isn't race illusory, deceptive? Shouldn't this mean something for the doing of racialism? Given the anthropological rejection of race, what does
this mean for the future of racial Indianhood?

In the first days of the Coop I saw the Closet Chickens as dedicated
adherents to racial Indianhood who might nevertheless one day awak-
en from the spell of race, like Richard Brautigan's Magic Child. Or would
the Chickens deliberately choose to go on being magic children?

In late May 2001 I flew to Boston and took a shuttle up to Dartmouth College, where two archaeologists, Joe Watkins and Deborah Nichols, had organized a conference called "On the Threshold: Native American–Archaeologist Relations in the Twenty-First Century." Joe had played a major role
in fostering the presence of Indians in archaeology during the 1990s. Now
it was the beginning of a new millennium, and Joe and Deborah thought
it seemed useful to bring together these new Indian archaeologists.

After the conference ended, one participant, Dorothy Lippert, got in
touch with everyone via group email. And through the following summer, we continued discussions that the conference had launched, nam-
ing ourselves the Closet Chickens. By summer's end, Desireé Martínez
had set us up as a Yahoo Group for easier communication.

In my first emails to the group, I brought up race as an issue, feeling that this topic lay at the heart of our deliberations. I'd been talking in a random way about race for maybe five years, but I still didn't feel very sure of what I ought to say about it. In fact, my efforts to explore race with others had proven somewhat disappointing.

"We're doing race," I'd note in a thoughtful tone that came off sounding tricky to people. "Should we be doing it if it isn't real?" I'd say this to colleagues and relatives. But it surprised and dismayed people and made them feel awkward to discuss what it meant that science had rejected race as a biological reality.

It seemed reasonable to me to question the doing of race, but my Indian relatives and my Indian colleagues didn't like it. We had all grown up learning how to do race and learning how to sort out the most socially desirable ways it should be done from the less desirable ways of doing it.

Most of the Indians I talked to were polite but firm. They had become quite good at being Indian and they enjoyed doing it. Whatever white science said about race, we Indians planned to keep improving the ways traditional racial Indianhood should be done and until the very end. In fact, my comments occasionally drew forth strong responses, defensive resentment. What I said about race sounded so outrageous to some people and their sense of self that it couldn't possibly be real. Was I serious?

I thought I'd get a better reception among Indians who were doing anthropology. As the Coop got going in the summer of 2001, I had high hopes that the Closet Chickens would start talking about the problem with race and we'd compare notes. Together we would help Indians and archaeologists figure out what it meant that race had been discredited as an explanation of human biological diversity. We would address the past, present, and future character of racial Indianhood. We wouldn't just be Indians; we would be Closet Chickens.

Cautiously excited about the possibilities, I sent my first email on race very soon after we began talking online. In this email I characterized the idea of being "Indian" / "Native American" as a fabrication of racial ideology, wholly dependent on the notion that people can be sorted out into races, and that race should be rejected as a false, inherently dehumanizing construction. The idea of race, I argued, creates a heavily edited identity which rudely shoves aside the historical processes that actually account for who we are. I invited the Chickens to ponder whether it is possible to accommodate race without embracing it.

Challenging race, I questioned the very foundation of the Coop's unifying identity as a group. The Chickens didn't respond with much enthusiasm. Polite replies sent by Chicken Noodle and Greasy Chicken expressed what quickly emerged as the consensus of the Coop. Rather than confront race, they wanted the warmth of trading ideas with other Indians, and finding friendship and mutual support—they wanted to bond through race.

Perhaps they needed time to sort out things. After all, I had taken several years to think about race and several more to get going on what it meant to reject it. Anyway, I looked forward to hearing their ideas about what we should say to each other in the Coop, and many interesting topics indeed arose.

In the months that followed, slowly my patience turned into disappointment as it became clear that Chickenry intended to proceed with racialism as their unifying identity, as the unwavering source of their social agenda. My comments jolted the Coop but didn't derail anyone from race. For the next three years, there would be no further discussion of my concerns about race.

With our new internet connection, it became convenient to begin expanding the membership. While the other Chickens scratched about looking for Indians to nominate in the fall of 2001, my first nominee was Chicken Nuggets. I wanted to know whether non-Indians would be welcome to join our deliberations. Nuggets had long ago become well-known in Indian country as a voice of reason among his colleagues in archaeology, trying to encourage more sensitivity and communication between Indians and archaeologists. If the Coop didn't accept Chicken Nuggets as a Chicken, then no white archaeologist would ever be truly welcome.

The Chickens readily agreed to admit Nuggets. Accepting him gave us a way to compromise. The enactment of racial Indianhood would proceed, but the Closet Chickens wouldn't become a racist Indians-Only project.

☜☞

As the beginning of the new century approached and appeared, I began trying to get my colleagues in the Native Arts Department at the Denver Art Museum to think about race. In early 2001 I took up the practice of circulating emails on the topic to the curator of the department and our other three colleagues. I included some of the Chicken chatter on race.

It had been my hope that the Chickens would help me with race and we'd look for new ideas and ways to proceed. And this would aid me in dealing with my colleagues at the Denver Art Museum. And if the Closet Chickens got going on race, and if the Denver Art Museum would join us... we would... we would—well, of course we would!

But the Chickens shied away from the issue.

Okay. Surely my anthropologist DAM colleagues would prove willing to sort out this issue with me. We could gradually build our own little network of supportive colleagues. Maybe we'd have to go ahead and keep doing race, but it would be a self-conscious enactment that would look for new angles and ask useful questions. Together we would struggle with race. I thought we could start with the name of our department, the Native Arts Department. The head of the department agreed to make this a topic for discussion.

So later on that year in September 2001, on the day after 9/11, my colleagues at DAM met to consider race and our departmental identity. In a somber mood, I said that the issue of race deserved thorough acknowledgment. We needed a useful exchange of ideas. I didn't have answers; I hoped instead for dialogue.

It was a short meeting. Favoring the proposition that what we did as a department was "ethnicity" rather than "race," my co-workers refused to acknowledge that race had anything to do with our department's racial identity. Deferring to the will of the majority, the head curator chose to do nothing. I had been outvoted.

By this time I had the impression that my colleagues were beginning to see me as a dubious contributor to the department. My work on NAGPRA was thorough and conscientious, but as an assistant curator my interests weren't very traditional. Looking for ways to confront our departmental mission of enacting bioracial Indianhood, I often wondered aloud whether we should collect German-made "Indian" artworks.

This seemed logical enough if we were truly bent on viewing Indian identity as pure ethnicity free of race-based biological authenticity tests. To my dismay, this suggestion of going so far as to actually treat Indianness as a non-biological cultural construction only served to further alienate my colleagues.

It seemed obvious to me that we were doing race as a department, and I suspected that we were now moving toward doing it as a covert operation under the cover of ethnicity. There didn't appear to be any interest in seeking other options. Aiming at challenging race, my departmental input necessarily came to be seen as very problematic.

By the beginning of fall 2001 as the leaves fell upon our various ideological positions in the Closet Chicken Coop and in the Native Arts Department, it became clear that my efforts to talk about race had failed. I had been courteously rebuffed. But I knew that the dubious nature of race invited questions that would never go away, and over the year that followed I kept looking for occasions to bring the topic up among the Chickens and at DAM.

Speaking at a Chicken session on "indigenous archaeology" at the spring 2002 annual meeting of the Society for American Archaeology, I discussed the problem of race. Chicken Nuggets followed. His comments sounded somewhat sympathetic to what I had just said. And he also included a strong statement of opposition to interpreting advocacy for racial indigenism as a call to replace white archaeologists with Indian archaeologists. Our comments, taken together, seemed to urge the Coop to confront the racial tenor of the emerging idea of indigenous archaeology.

Mother Clucker opened her presentation by observing that she had no idea how to respond to what she had just heard. I took this as an acknowledgment that my challenge to race posed a profound problem for Chickens who intended to bond through racial Indianhood. She seemed disturbed at the possibility that the Coop might back off from race as the unifying source of communal identity. Would the Chickens one day decline to bond as Indians? If these were indeed her fears that day, time has proven them unfounded.

At DAM I joined a special committee formed to envision the development of new exhibit spaces for the Native Arts Department, and I made a determined pitch for re-conceptualizing our departmental acceptance of race. This led to some lively discussions. But it gradually became clear that no one knew what to do and no one felt particularly motivated to figure things out. My colleagues soon drew together in unified resistance to my pressure, patiently turning aside all my ideas on race. By the fall of 2002 an impasse evolved as I persisted in suggesting that we do something and they quietly listened.

Finally one morning in December 2002 the curator of my department stopped into my office to inform me that the museum administrator in charge of the committee didn't wish to go to bat for my ideas with DAM administrators and the Board. The committee operated as a good team and worked well together. With my radical notion of challenging race, I didn't fit. Thinking back now, our differences of opinion were sharp but respectful.

To be sure, my observations about race had daunting implications. Would anyone at the Denver Art Museum support making big changes in the way we did race? Could the museum initiate meaningful change and still keep the goodwill of its racialized constituents? I was alone in wanting to find answers to these interesting questions.

ల౧

With the end of that millennium and the beginning of the next thousand years, it seemed like a good time for everyone to rethink old assumptions. But in the early years of that propitious time, nothing changed with regard to race. Everyone I knew would go on doing it. In fact, the Closet Chickens and my department at the Denver Art Museum all came to share a single mind on the issue of race.

The challenge to race as a biological construction wasn't an issue that people wanted to dwell on. No one particularly wanted to confront the racial assumptions that guided their lives. Everyone agreed that it was both convenient and desirable to keep perpetuating racialism rather than consider ways to defuse it.

The world had long empowered race, and people felt understandably doubtful that the world would ever agree to disempower race. Giving me a fair hearing on my own terms, my fringe notion of raising some kind of systematic challenge to race struck everyone as unrealistic, impossible. Anyway, many other important matters needed attention.

I sensed a certain amount of milling about as if people might be taking sides, but everyone just needed time to sort out how they felt about my comments. In the end, during those days at the beginning of the new era to come, none of my colleagues decided that they shared my concerns. Little productive dialogue ensued. After that, continuing my efforts to keep the challenge to race alive served merely to harden opposition to my notions.

I had confronted race and had been defeated.

When the holidays ended, in January 2003 I submitted my resignation from my job as an assistant curator at the Denver Art Museum. It had become difficult for me to see how I could contribute to the departmental program—I didn't relish the thought of looking on, ignored, while the museum built new exhibits around the old idea of race. I would give thought on my own time to what I should say about race and what should happen next.

Wouldn't We Wouldn't We Wouldn't

In the fourth year of the third millennium of the Common Era, I made astonishing progress in spreading the news about race, but the year didn't begin very well. On the first day of that year the first thing I did was to send an email to the Closet Chickens with an attachment that talked about race. And somehow, for reasons that aren't clear, this move had the effect of completely shutting down some very exciting chatter in the Coop about an idea proposed by Chicken Noodle.

Not long before the winter solstice of the third year of the third millennium, she had suggested launching a new professional organization for Indian archaeologists. Hearing the idea, the Chickens had chattered excitedly, and they all had things to say. I collected the excitement and put it into a document for easy reference, thinking it would be a convenient resource as the Coop made itself into something else.

I'd been silent during the chatter, thinking about what kind of role my thinking on race should play. I finally decided that I'd make a pitch to have the new organization put race on its official agenda in some form. Maybe they'd do a website and invite me to help shape a component on race.

They'd at least do that, wouldn't they?

Instead, Chicken Noodle's dream died suddenly in the January 2004 snows. I felt like maybe I'd taken an axe and chopped its head off. There might have been a few more flaps and maybe some scurrying in the snow before the dream keeled over and the winter buried it forever. I hadn't intended for that to happen. But in any case, Noodle's suggestion didn't go anywhere after that.

☉☉

So in the first cold winter months of the year, my oldest brother, a lawyer at the Native American Rights Fund, sent an email to me, Suzan Harjo, Tex Hall, and James Riding In. Did anyone have useful ideas on what to do in response to the Kennewick Man court decision? This court decision gutted the consultation provisions of the Native American Graves Protection and Repatriation Act, dismissed oral traditions on the basis of a selectively slanted ultra-conservative analysis, and made it impossible for ancient human remains to be classified as "Native American."

I explained to my brother that I was opposed to bestowing race upon Kennewick Man and his peers, but that the National Park Service cultural affiliation findings for Kennewick Man were flawed because they ignored readily available information that I had published in 2000. They'd used my publication, but they had ignored what it meant. I had made a case for ancient connections of my Caddoan ancestors to Kennewick Man—in the parlance of NAGPRA, Kennewick Man has a likely cultural affiliation with the Pawnee Nation.

Months later I learned that NARF had decided to take on Suzan Harjo, James Riding In, and several others as clients. This group soon led the way in pushing Congress to amend NAGPRA to ensure that the statute's racial definition for "Native American" would apply to ancient human remains.

This choice of strategy offered itself as a practical course of action. An entire class of American race-based sovereignties had something at stake in this issue, and during the late twentieth century, adherents to racial Indianhood had become very sophisticated at advancing their political and cultural agendas by tapping into the social power of race. Defending the idea that all America should maintain allegiance to the idea of racial identity and help uphold the tenets of racial Indianhood, practitioners of race moved to keep NAGPRA and the American legal system faithful to the production of race.

From the perspective of Indian political activism, my research-oriented approach to the Kennewick problem—that is, investigating oral traditions and archaeology to divine the connections of Kennewick Man to the Pawnee Nation—lacked any appeal to racial bonding and did not readily lend itself toward furtherance of a more general racial political agenda. Choosing a race-based solution over research into cultural affiliation, a more sweeping impact could be advanced on behalf of Indian country. This experience served as a reminder to me that even though the ideology of race originated as an import from colonialist Europe, racial Indianhood is nevertheless treated by Indians as indispensably indigenous to America.

෨෧

In the years since this incident, I have often wondered whether the race-based political mechanisms that sustain the category of "Indian" sovereignties in the United States also serve to prevent those nations from ever regaining full sovereign status as independent nations.

I think the answer is that antiquated notions of race not only dehumanize Indian people, investment in racialism and the racial status of "Indian tribes" also acts as a substitute for truly advancing the restoration of independent nationhood. Hoping to preserve their various cultural identities, when Indian tribes embrace racial Indianhood and declare allegiance to American racialism, they sacrifice any hope of regaining full political independence in favor of sustaining their race-based niches in the American empire.

It is arguable that no practical alternative exists for this situation, and that the tenets of racial Indianhood help to protect the remaining shreds of nationhood among Indian tribes in the United States. It is also reasonable to suggest that before we can reject race, we must devise a practical social justice counter-narrative to racial Indianhood—an alternative that can realistically take the place of racial empowerment, serve social justice, and permit the dismantling of the social structures that uphold race.

What would such a counter-narrative to race look like? Is it possible to construct a convincing alternative narrative that is more socially just than the social justice promoted via racial empowerment? Any such a counter-narrative, I presume, must begin by suggesting some kind of strategic realignment of the powers of racial Indianhood away from race and toward... what?

Delivering the news about the scientific rejection of race in an America that is gradually becoming caught up in rethinking race, is this bad news for Indians? Or is it an opportunity of some kind?

☙

I had once been an Indian and I understood the attraction and power of the bond of racial Indianhood. What was I now?

Well, I'd given up race, but I hadn't given up being a Pawnee. I was still a Pawnee, wasn't I? Thinking about this question, I knew that the Pawnees today believe in race and see themselves not just as Pawnees, but as Pawnee Indians. And as a historian I also knew that this hadn't always been the case.

Race had come among my Pawnee ancestors and had convinced them to become Indians. Race didn't ever encourage them to ever think of this as optional. Instead, race told the Pawnees that it was an inflexible authoritarian law of nature. I inherited this idea as part of the tradition of being Pawnee, a tradition handed down from my Pawnee ancestors. We are Pawnees—Pawnee Indians.

And in the spring of 2004 the Field Museum of Natural History contacted me for advice about their Pawnee earthlodge lecture program. The head of the anthropology department wanted to kill the lecture—he had an axe in his hand and was ready to chop off its head when they called me. The earthlodge lecture program was popular with the public and the Education Department preferred to keep it alive.

Would this be a good place to talk about race? I decided to find out.

I wrote up a detailed outline that looked at Pawnee history and the development of racial identity. I emailed it to the anthropologist they'd hired to develop a new program. I said to myself: they're an anthropology museum; surely they're already doing something on race. Talking to a group of staff on the phone, I explained the project. I thought I did a pretty good job.

But they didn't like it. It seemed too complicated. They would instead rely on Martha Blaine's books on Pawnee history for material. If you ever visit this famous anthropology museum, if they happen to be doing something interesting on the topic of race, they're probably not doing it in their Pawnee earthlodge.

☯

That year wore on. Spring gradually gave way to summer. My oldest brother's oldest son got married. Summer deepened. And in mid-August I attended Wayne and Laurie Moore's 2004 Summer Party.

I've known Wayne since we met as students in the creative writing program at the University of Colorado in 1975. I've kept in touch with Wayne over the years since then, and after the beginning of the new millennium Wayne and Laurie began holding an annual summer party at their home in the country not far from Haystack Mountain in Boulder County.

Sitting on their patio in August 2004, I had a chat on race with one of my most important mentors, Jenny Dorn. Jenny has been publishing my work since the early 1980s, encouraging me to write and be a writer, so I have treasured her friendship for years even when we haven't kept in touch. Her dead husband, Ed Dorn, had been a leading literary light upon the Boulder scene, a respected author of both epic lyrical poems and verse concisions. I had stood nearby during the 1980s as the two of them and their many friends assembled *Rolling Stock* and published my work.

So Jenny listened very patiently to the things I said about race. When I finished she had a thoughtful look in her eyes. Conceding that I might indeed have a good point, Jenny nevertheless suspected that endorsing my views might well pose some kind of threat to her husband's legacy. Ed had written very movingly about Indians and white people.

Jenny was not idly dismissing my words. Instead, living in a racial world, we must do our best to work with what the world gives us, and Jenny's rational response reflected a lifetime of wise and compassionate experience with the realities of race. On a more personal level, I had put her in a rather awkward position by advocating a viewpoint that might well have the effect of making her husband's lifelong labors appear somewhat anachronistic. It seemed polite to let the matter drop.

A short time later I found myself repeating my standard conversation on race with my old creative writing professor, Peter Michelson—another editor of *Rolling Stock*—and his girlfriend, Judith Aplon. Much to my amazement, they both grasped very quickly my point about race not being a valid concept. In the lively discussion that followed, they seemed unconscious of how unusual their response to me might be in the world—maybe this was the kind of irrational response that the colossal rationale of race needed.

Peter encouraged me to get moving on writing something about this.

"Get moving on a fucking book, Roger!" he advised.

After the party, I began writing short vignettes on my experiences with the issue of race. I wrote three or four of these things over the next few weeks and this material grew into a booklet and then into a whole fucking book on race. I got the title for *The Magic Children* from a little story I published in Jenny Dorn's 2004 issue of *Square One*. And I feel a sense of warmth from the fact that this story tells of something that happened long ago when I lived with my oldest brother and his family, back when I was an Indian. I treasure the warmth we had then as a family.

At the end of the 1990s and at the beginning of the next millennium, many people whom I love and respect heard my views on race and chose to continue doing it. Their choice was without rancor; none of them wished me any ill will.

As they saw it, race might not be real biologically, but perhaps nothing should change culturally. The truths of race seemed irrelevant to the familiar reality of its practice. And their reasons for doing race were diverse and strongly held—racial identity gets wielded in the world like a precious natural resource, even if it isn't natural. Letting go of race wouldn't ever be a simple matter of one day making a decision. Rather than aim at somehow changing people's hearts, it seemed more realistic to aim at giving everyone a choice.

෧෧

That year as 2004 proceeded through winter, then spring, and on toward the end of summer, I often gave thought to the Closet Chickens. While experimenting with vignettes on race, I thought it might be useful to follow this same model in my emails to the Chickens, creating what would be essentially a sporadic column on race. In the Coop I would figure out how to talk about race.

In early September 2004, Chicken Noodle circulated a newspaper report that referred to the Kennewick Man situation and the study of ancient skulls. The Chickens responded in their usual way, talking as if race were something real, something they intended to perpetuate. I couldn't keep silent. On September 7, I sent an email that challenged race—would this prove to be another commentary they could dismiss?

But something was in the air. Checking my emails on September 9, I saw that a number of Chickens had responded. Chicken Nuggets, Cackle Hu-Yolk, and Chicken Claws all chimed in with emails that expressed support for developing a critical perspective on race. This was the first time the Chickens as a group had responded with open sympathy for my views on race.

Cackle soon came up with a plan to publish a group of papers as a special issue in the *American Indian Quarterly*, and Nuggets volunteered to write up something based on our email exchange. He asked for my help and I agreed. Long ago at the end of the 1980s I had once-upon-a-time asked for his help and he had immediately agreed. And that had been during a time when few others in American archaeology would help me do the things I thought needed to be done.

If Chicken Nuggets wanted me to help him, of course I'd help.

On the first day of 2005 I received the first draft of the paper and we launched into preparation of "Beyond Racism: Some Opinions about Racialism and American Archaeology." Seeking to update and contextualize familiar discourse on racial Indian people versus racial white people—now repositioned under the terminological rubric of "Indigenous peoples" versus "Western" colonialism—Cackle Hu-Yolk designed the special issue to focus on the idea of decolonizing archaeology. "Beyond Racism" would appear near the end. It suggested that we needed to move beyond challenging racism into challenging race itself.

In the end, I felt very pleased with the fourth year of the third millennium. With the sound of Peter Michelson's enthusiastic encouragement echoing in my ears, I'd begun writing what ultimately became a whole fucking book on the topic of race.

And I kept hearing in my head how Chicken Nuggets had spoken out in support of my views. And with his help we'd had a major conversation among the Closet Chickens about race, and Nuggets and I had consequently written a solid paper on the topic, and maybe this would be the beginning of something new and good in our little Coop. Now we would talk about race in a more complicated way and we would compare notes and share our experiences and together we would develop a useful analysis of race.

And as we Chickens would help each other figure out race, together we would help change the way everyone looks at race. Together we would ponder the future of race here at the dawn of the new millennium, wouldn't we?

Wouldn't we?

Is Race Good?

From: Sweet & Sour Ugly Duckling (formerly Sweet & Sour Chicken)
Date: July 20, 2005
To: closetchicken listserv

Chicken Noodle, I understand your impulse to joke about my approach to race. And I appreciate your effort to find a candid yet inoffensive way to respond to views that must offend you.

Looking around the Coop, I sometimes get the feeling that I don't really fit in, though you and the others have been very accommodating. Perhaps I'm less of a Chicken and more of an Ugly Duckling!

☙❧

When pressed, most people want to see race as a good thing because it's so powerfully present in their lives and holds such compelling personal meaning. Why confront or give up a good thing? But most people aren't aware that race is, in reality, an optional cultural choice rather than an inherent biological condition. What would these unsuspecting victims of race do, if given a conscious, truly informed choice on the matter? Whatever the answer, people deserve a chance to make their own decisions.

This may or may not be an interesting question for Chickenry, but it at least seems useful to raise a related and more pertinent set of questions: Is race a good thing for archaeology? Isn't there some kind of dilemma involved in just accepting race as an unquestioned foundation for archaeological scholarship? Acceptance of the contention that race has been discredited ought to have meaningful implications for the future practice of racialism throughout the academy.

As a matter of morality, knowing race is a cultural choice rather than an unshakable biological imperative, and knowing that race distorts the nature of our humanity, surely we must weigh in our hearts whether we believe race is something that makes our world a better place. Indulging in a vast fib, even if you think of it as a little white lie, can't be good for archaeology or scholarship of any kind. Race persists in the academy because academic racialists have power, not because race is a good idea.

Other points of view on this issue no doubt exist—what are they? If Chickendom doesn't take this topic seriously as a relevant matter for anthropological archaeology, who will?

When people know the choice to be made and choose to go on doing race, I suspect it's because they wisely grasp the fact that our world isn't ready to really let people choose. Race is too powerful; it can't be denied its place of preeminence in our lives.

☉☉

Delphine Red Shirt once published a comment in the *American Indian Quarterly* in which she complained of her treatment at the hands of *Indian Country Today* and then observed in essence: Who would dare to give up practicing race? Not me, she declared. The implication is that we have no choice but to go on doing what we do when we employ scholarship as a way to enliven the visible and invisible assumptions of race.

I think there is an alternative—an ultimate punchline to the dizzy practical joke that race pulls on our humanity. This alternative to the status quo is to talk about the meaning of race in our lives, to encourage a range of discourse, and to create the explicit possibility of genuinely optional choices for people. At least, there should be an alternative of this sort.

If Delphine Red Shirt suspects it isn't quite rational to think of eluding the clutches of race, perhaps she is right to feel cynicism on this point as long as academic intellectuals like the Closet Chickens find efforts like mine to be tiresome, hardly worth the effort of even bothering to come up with a good joke at my expense.

☉☉

No doubt most of the people we love in the world are unaware of the choice to be made about race and their plan is to just pass race along intact into the future and. . . . And in time some people might well appreciate knowing that there is an alternative to the terribly fun hilarity of race.

It may be presumptuous of me to assume that Chickenry as a group has a special obligation to give people this power to choose. But I believe that archaeology should be anthropological, and it should be attentive to complex cultural and historical circumstances—this is, after all, the inherent ethos of groups like the World Archaeological Congress and laws like the Native American Graves Protection and Repatriation Act. This assumption, anyway, is what drives me to sweeten or sour the Coop's soup with emails like this one, Chicken Noodle. . . .

S&S

Through Vine's Looking Glass, Darkly

Dreaming my "third bear dream" long ago in 1975, I encountered three huge bears. Driving in Saskatchewan with two friends, we came to the end of a faint forest road. Three huge bears charged out of the underbrush, each one the size of our little jeep. We jumped out and ran back down the road to a dark lake. The giant bears galloped after us.

They caught my two friends, but I dived into deep water, and…

And I didn't escape either.

☜

From: Sweet & Sour Chicken
Date: November 24, 2005
To: closetchicken listserv

Visiting my nephew's house one day, I noticed he had painted a small portrait of Vine Deloria Jr. and had hung it in his dining room. Vine's smile beamed warm colors down into the room, a cheerful air. I paused to study the face in the picture. At my elbow my nephew spoke softly. Vine Deloria deserves honor among Indians, said my nephew. And this painting will appear in a magazine soon, he said, a special issue honoring Deloria.

That's cool, I said to him. And I meant it. I felt pleased with my nephew's success as an artist.

Vine Deloria Jr. was a major figure—a giant—in the doings of twentieth century racial Indianhood. In over thirty books and innumerable commentaries, Deloria effectively articulated many of the key tenets of late twentieth century racial Indianhood, focusing particularly on the construction of racial nationalism and sovereignty, and the character of racial Indian religious and cultural ideology.

At Deloria's death in the fall of 2005 he received many glowing tributes from racial Indians and others—tributes that remarked on his quite remarkable influence and stature in Indian country. My nephew's warm portrait echoed these warm sentiments. Vine would be missed among all the Indians in Indian country.

As I looked from the painting to my nephew, I could see in his eyes his sincere appreciation for Deloria. Painting this portrait with his heart, it was his way of acknowledging and honoring a real giant in the production of late twentieth century racial Indianhood.

My own feelings were… well, I had never really sat down to sort out in any systematic way how I felt about Vine Deloria. Maybe because it wasn't very pleasant the way things had gone between the two of us all those years ago. It hadn't actually been all that long ago, but it seemed like another lifetime to me. Back when I was an Indian. Back when I believed in race and it believed in me.

When Vine Deloria died all the Closet Chickens took note, and a flurry of notices scrawled across the list. I sent in several links. A tribute by Rick Williams, a comment by Phil Deloria. The chatter was solemn and respectful. The Chickens respected Vine. He had inspired many members of the coop.

Back in the early 1990s Rick and I had been students at the University of Colorado. Rick's warmth and interest in people was genuine, and he got along very well with Vine. And in 1994 Vine's son Phil had come to the history department at CU and I shifted from working with Vine to working with Phil in my final days as a graduate student. Phil was a pleasure to study with. Thoughtful, diplomatic, very helpful and encouraging.

I was pleased to pass along to the Coop the thoughts of Phil and Rick, Vine's son and a close friend. I kept my own thoughts to myself.

But when one of the Chickens made a negative comment about a critic of Deloria, I thought I might say something. Maybe I'd try to figure out how I felt about what happened all those years ago in another lifetime when I was an Indian and when I knew Vine Deloria. What did all that mean?

When Vine first appeared at the University of Colorado in the early 1990s, the history department put him in charge of my upcoming master's program as my advisor and the chair of my thesis committee. My thinking had taken shape in the course of doing pre-NAGPRA repatriation research. Working as a consultant to the Native American Rights Fund and the Pawnee Nation, I had begun exploring how oral traditions could be used as evidence about Pawnee historical connections to ancestral populations. Even so, by the time I started my new academic program at CU, I'd already encountered hostility from various Indian intellectuals for my use of archaeological evidence— hostility based on the idea that moral objections to white archaeology should serve as a tenet of Indian racial allegiance.

Thinking that my research had great potential for shedding useful light on ancient historical settings, I felt confident. Vine was an academic scholar, so I knew I could earn his support. I pictured how he would become interested in my work and his support would open minds among Indians who thought well of him and who would listen to what he'd say about my work. My logic seemed clear and strong and surely Vine would see that. Together we would find important things to talk about and he would help me in my work.

In my first meeting with Vine, I had lunch with him and several professors from the CU department of history. Vine spoke of his interest in "geomythology." It sounded promising. Maybe we'd have some common interests, something with which we could build a good working relationship. I had many research ideas and things I wanted to look at for my thesis on origin stories. Now I spent many hours excitedly thinking that with Vine's help I would show everyone how archaeological scholarship and the study of oral traditions could be performed together. From such materials, I would invent "ancient Indian history." Maybe Vine would get excited about it too. Maybe he'd be a big help.

Getting wind of my notions over time, Vine wanted to know where I might be going with all this. In our first discussions, it became immediately clear to me that he didn't share my enthusiasm. He had a definite vision of the way things should be done, a vision crafted in the course of his long advocacy for empowering racial Indianhood. He tried to get me headed down the path he thought best for an Indian student, for the production of a racially Indian scholarship.

But the things he thought I should know didn't seem very helpful to me. He warned me, for example, that I would be aiding and abetting the cultural enemies of Indian country, the ones who had bedeviled his thinking for many years since the 1970s and before. The Wounded Knee trials came up several times as he harangued against my approach to archaeology. I would be helping his long-fought enemies, he said to me. Indians should do battle with white archaeology and deter the anti-Indian doings of white archaeologists. To buy into archaeology would be seriously detrimental to my career. He said many such things to me, all expressing his disappointment with my thinking.

Okay, I wouldn't get his help. Declining to help me do my scholarship, would he actively oppose me? Could I still do what I thought I needed to do?

One incident made me especially wary. Working out my ideas about the significance of the theme of darkness in stories of dark underworlds was a crucial component of my analysis, pointing, I thought, to very ancient historical events in origin stories. I thought I saw history where others saw metaphor and myth. It meant that—as I saw it then—Indian origin stories held glimpses of history going back millennia. Standing in his office one day, Vine pressed me to articulate what I thought the theme of darkness meant.

I knew it would be touchy because my historical interpretation of the theme pointed to an association with the Arctic Circle and the Bering Strait.

Vine was horrified. He explained that I'd be making a big mistake. Indians wouldn't sit still for it, and even academics would, he predicted, come to reject the whole Bering Strait thing within the next ten years anyway. He couldn't in good conscience help me go down that path, the wrong track.

Then he shared with me some of his own ideas. Reliance on academic scholarship and science would be misguided, he said. I should be open to more esoteric possibilities. He pondered the likelihood that maybe people came to the Americas through a realm of darkness, but via UFOs, maybe even coming from some other star system. He urged me to consider studying this alternative to the Bering Strait. I needed to cull through the so-called fringe literature for the really important obscure truths, he said. Now this, Roger, would be a courageous thing to do, he said.

His response disappointed me greatly. We both felt very disappointed, wary. It wasn't easy to communicate after that.

Toward the end of our time together, it became clear that Vine didn't like my choice of one of my thesis committee members. An archaeologist. The single occasion when I got everyone together for a meeting, Vine sat there in thunderous silence as I talked.

Sensing Vine's mood, I decided to mention a certain mysterious spiritual experience I'd had in the mid-1970s. In what I call my "third bear dream" I dreamed of three huge bears. Launching into my research on oral traditions and the end of the Pleistocene, I came across an artist's depiction of the mighty short-faced bear. I felt stunned seeing it. It resembled the three bears in my third dream. I wondered whether that dream might somehow be related to my present work. Mulling over that question before the committee, I saw how Vine's expression didn't soften. My dreams meant nothing to him.

Finally he interrupted. He had something he wanted to say. He turned to the archaeologist sitting next to him, and, looming over him in a threatening way, proceeded to bomb him into the stone age. Vine suspected that the archaeologist had something to do with my warped un-Indian thinking. Finishing his ugly tirade, Vine declared, "I've had enough of this; you guys go on without me!" He shoved away from the table angrily and stalked from the room.

Thinking back, that might have been the last time I ever saw Vine. The message seemed clear enough. I talked to another committee member about replacing him. Would such a thing be possible? It turned out that when she checked with Vine, he had suddenly become too busy with other commitments to continue with my thesis committee.

I went on to complete my thesis at the end of 1994, working with Phil Deloria. It's on origin stories and the anthropology of Indian origins, and I'm proud of that work. In recognition of my work on oral traditions and archaeology, CU awarded me a master's degree in history with an emphasis in ancient Indian history. So far as I know, no one else in this star system or any other has ever gotten such a degree.

☜☞

Vine made reference once to a book he planned to write someday. This happened in a class he was teaching. He gave a brief speech. He would drive a stake through many ridiculous archaeological theories, he vowed. This vague comment was the only time he ever mentioned in my presence that he was at work on what would become *Red Earth, White Lies*.

At the end of 1995 or early 1996 I came across *Red Earth, White Lies* in a bookstore. Reading it, I felt sad. It seemed to me that Vine had treated my thesis research as raw material.

I guess he always did feel that I wasn't doing justice to those Indian oral traditions. Now in this book he took care to show everyone how those oral traditions ought to be properly viewed. My way of thinking about ancient history stood in complete opposition to his view of the Indian past. Why had I ever thought to sway him? It seemed a naive notion.

Reading the book later, I found it had some interesting stuff in it, very thoughtful and beautifully written. But overall I'm glad he didn't acknowledge me in any way. He took the material I'd been looking at and he had his own things to say about it. It didn't sound like me at all.

In this book, Vine articulated a powerful message for faithful practitioners of racial Indianhood, a message to all Indian country. The idea of being Indian held a central place in Vine's thinking. He thought long and deeply on racial Indianhood—what it should do in the world, what it should think, what it should look like. *Red Earth, White Lies* speaks his mind on such matters. Treating origin stories as received wisdom—while borrowing from science in a highly selective way—constituted a fundamental statement of racial allegiance. Red Pride guided what adherents to racial Indianhood should make of their origin stories.

☜☞

Seeing the Chicken chatter about Vine and their heartfelt gratitude and warm acknowledgment, I saw how Vine Deloria had an influential place in the Coop. An inspiration he was, a guiding thinker. On his path they traveled, the Closet Chickens. He was gone now, but they would keep going.

The Chickens didn't seem to know how Vine really felt. As evidence of this, the Chickens had been willing to listen to me. Vine hadn't been willing. To be sure, it wasn't as if the Chickens were willing to go with me down my path very much farther than Vine had been willing to go, but they were polite about it. Vine had limits to his patience with me. Some of the Chickens wanted to hear what I had to say; Vine had no reason to bother with me.

Surely Vine wouldn't have wanted to serve as the intellectual inspiration for the Closet Chickens, a Great Red Rooster. I felt sure of this. He wouldn't want such credit. In fact, he would shove away from that table angrily and stalk out of such a horribly offensive chatroom.

Wouldn't he?

Thinking this, I mulled over what it meant. I had failed to find a way to win Vine's goodwill, his support all those years ago. Reading *Red Earth, White Lies*, I thought the book positioned itself to advance the cause of Indian anti-science anti-archaeology intellectualism and Indian race-based cultural separatism.

As I see it, in fact, following Vine's leadership the politics of racial polarity has continued to dominate discourse among Indians about archaeology. He succeeded in passing along his vision of that world to the next generation of Indians in Indian country. He had an opportunity to help change things, to seek the kind of partnership and mutual respect that I espoused in my work, but he thought it wise to reject this approach.

It's true, however, that Vine might well have been willing to bestow his blessing on Cackle Hu-Yolk's paradigm of "decolonizing archaeology." Particularly if those words mean showing white non-indigenous archaeos to the door and replacing them with red indigenous… well, not red indigenous archaeos, but red indigenous academics of some kind.

The idea of decolonizing archaeology might appeal to him, but it seems more likely to me that Vine would have regarded Chickenry with a sense of dismay, if not outright horror. A dedicated and passionate advocate of anti-colonial pro-Indian ultra-tribal-indigenous-nationalism, Vine was an Indian super-patriot. In his separatist vision of racial Indianism, Indians could bond through opposition to the white intellectual superstructures of colonialist archaeology.

This doesn't leave much room for partnership between red Indians and white archaeology. I got the feeling that a majority of Chickens thought they could follow Vine's leadership and yet somehow see themselves as promoting partnership between Indian country and archaeology. However much Chickenry might appreciate Vine Deloria, I felt pretty certain that Vine would not have reciprocated. He'd surely feel very cool, if not downright chilly, toward the Coop. And he for sure wouldn't stand still for being dubbed the Great Red Rooster of Chickendom.

Thinking of all the things I felt about Vine Deloria, we might arguably seek to sort out the personal from the professional. At a personal level it was certainly difficult for me to feel very much gratitude. He had lumped me in among his enemies. He didn't want to work with me. At a professional level, Vine's opposition wasn't informative in any usefully critical way. For him, the dictates of allegiance to racial Indianhood demanded that Indian intellectuals confront archaeology, not buy into it. Proposing, as I did, to engage in archaeological scholarship for my thesis project, Vine suggested that I had sold out to the sworn enemies of racial Indianhood.

In his mind, such situations might summon forth a certain amount of useful critical analysis, but he didn't shy away from opportunities for witty name-calling and clever racial smearing. Oddly enough, I understand this response. Objective scholarship and liberal courtesy in advancing professional debate are laudable standards even though dispassionate research is never done just with the mind—it is invariably done the way we do things with our hearts. But personal attacks are not deployed for the purpose of contributing to useful criticism. Instead, they have functional usage in shaping the politics that embed the production of scholarship.

In challenging race with my mind and heart, I always understand that I challenge the way people do race with their minds and hearts. This must always be acknowledged when we consider what kind of dialogue to have about race.

∞

It's interesting to ponder Vine's view of me and my professional aspirations now that I have given up race. As a professor, in the courses I had with him, he was a well-informed racial ideologue in his class lectures, speaking in eloquent depth about the historical oppression of Indians by whites and how that history relates to contemporary life. In those days, of course, I lacked the anti-race non-racial analytical perspective that now provides me with a lens through which to view such racialism.

Dismissing my point of view and knowing little of my personal history, Vine seemed to think that I had too much interest in conducting academic research and not enough willingness to tailor my agenda to promote race-based social justice. Whatever the accuracy of this evaluation, maybe Vine at least had the gist of it, a foretelling of my future state of mind. To some degree, it is arguable that he saw in me someone who didn't feel the proper kind of enthusiasm for the agenda of racial loyalty, of loyalty to the racial agenda of Red Pride.

In those days, in fact, I had already embraced the idea of valuing multicultural common ground. Conjoining archaeological evidence and oral traditions, I had already set forth upon a quest for some form of racially transcendent academic narrative. And today, for sure, I reject the idea of taking pride in racial loyalty. It's a racist thing to do. I have come to see that the whole idea of doing race the way Vine did it—and the way we all grew up doing it—is a bad idea.

Most people seem to think race can be benign, or even a good thing to do. Maybe we can change from treating race as biological to treating it as cultural. Maybe. I listen carefully when I sense that people are trying to make these points. So far I'm unconvinced. Since racialism in all its forms distorts the nature of our humanity, race is inherently objectionable. At its best it is merely less repugnant than blatant unilateral racism, its truly repugnant offspring.

Even so, seeing how racialists in the academy and in the world beyond do bioracialism today, I can't really picture those same people doing race as pure culture. Racial Indianhood yields up a ready source of social power only so long as it is treated as if it tells an exclusive biological truth, a truth limited to people with putative "Indian blood."

But we should have choices. We should have the choice of doing race as culture and the choice of forgoing race in its entirety. And some people, no matter what happens, will never let go of treating race as a biological reality. When we do whatever comes next in this story, we must find ways to wish one another well, because it won't be easy for any of us. Some of us will feel alone. Afraid. Uncertain of our certainties.

A vast social reality stands up in our midst, in our world. The culture of race sustains this reality, the way we do things with our hearts and our minds.

Race is everywhere in our way of life. That's certain.

And Vine Deloria stands up at the pinnacle of the historical ideology of racial Indianhood. He stands for doing race and for handing it on intact. He devoted his life to this proposition.

I reject this agenda. Race is not a good thing. I want to be polite about it, but in the end I push my chair away from that table; I don't want a seat at that table anymore. You must go on with your meeting without me.

☙

It isn't easy to sort out such things, I know. Yet it seems important.

It is certainly fitting to honor the accomplishments of our predecessors, and I agree with my nephew: Vine Deloria Jr.'s achievements deserve acknowledgment. But we are nevertheless free to raise issues that challenge the world as we know it, and to question the social realities that stand up in our midst.

What do you think, Chickens? When you look at portraits of Vine Deloria, your fabled Great Red Rooster of Chickendom... when you study the way his smile beams its colors down upon the people, beaming down from his colorful past into your... future....

Looking inside yourself under that glow, where do you stand?

S&S

☙

Deep inside myself in this dream. At the bottom of the lake. I found things in the mud to grasp. The bear swam overhead. Looking. . . . Looking for me. The water churned angrily. Its burning face, its burning claws.
I had no choice. I rose to meet them.
I closed my eyes.

The Past, Destiny's Chicken

From: Sweet & Sour Chicken
Date: February 24, 2006
To: closetchicken listserv

Earlier today I happened to find myself reading an essay by Steven Weinberg in his book of essays, *Facing Up*. In this particular essay he honors Galileo by pondering the nature of time—a fascinating excursion through the ways modern physics has wrestled with time.

Weinberg's conclusion is that although time is a concept that can't be pinned down in any definitive way, it most clearly will not be settled "through the arguments of philosophy or theology." He takes the position that we must look to "mathematical theories based on observation" for the means to eventually settle the matter.

Toward this end, I'm particularly intrigued with the ideas of other physicists like Jim Hartle and Stephen Hawking, though my grasp of the issues is thin. People typically think of time in terms of what Weinberg characterizes as "an inexorable succession of instants that make an absolute separation between past and future," but time seems to be something more complex and elusive.

This has gradually become important to me as a student of oral history/oral traditions, because time is the unspoken invisible medium through which such narratives and our sense of narrative can be said to exist. In seeking to account for ourselves and in performing our versions of selfhood—and in creating explanatory models that can be shared with others—the common definition of time as articulated by Weinberg seems taken for granted by everyone. But this doesn't really account for the ways that memory and narrative actually operate. In other words, maybe we need to pay attention to what the physicists are saying.

As a tenet of racial Indianhood, it's often said that "Indians" conceive of time in a non-linear way, usually portrayed as "circular" in structure. The idea of course is to build a racially based impenetrable wall between "linear-thinking" white people and "circular-thinking" Indians. I've never quite grasped what this strategy means beyond the obvious appeal to racial bonding.

It is interesting, nevertheless, to put forward more than one way to characterize the nature of time because it at least complicates the simplistic popular notion of "linear time"—the same "linear" form that I suggest is not sufficient in explaining the medium that gives life to oral narrative and the contingent evolution of individual and communal forms of selfhood. If we drop the unhelpful rhetorical appeal to race, perhaps we can search for some better way to express what happens when we humans create stories about ourselves, drawing upon memory in the medium of time to portray what we've done and who we think we are when we do the things we do in our lives.

Now that I mention it, in thinking about such esoterica, I suppose this is where I seem to be going in some sense with my recent focus on personal narrative and my study of oral documents and what can be said about "the past." Situating myself within the narrative in a conscious way—having a personal viewpoint somewhere in the stories I tell to explain the world—has been a useful way to get into the development of a different kind of "history."

In this effort, I'm interested in how Pawnee traditional conceptualizations of the past seem to imply that time should be viewed in terms of a kind of borderless periodization in which complex relationships between cause and effect give rise to human and celestial history. This history is characterized by a kind of mirroring effect in which timeless immortal celestial doings foreshadow the mortal chronology of human events. In this system of thought, both linearity and circularity are too simplistic to serve as independent explanations for what happens in time and the ways we situate our views of ourselves.

In other words, maybe things will ultimately only add up if we take seriously the idea of seeking to formulate and understand useful "mathematical theories based on observation" rather than counting too much on theories that draw exclusively upon "the arguments of philosophy or theology." For this reason, I look forward to the complex integrative task of reconfiguring my identity and narratives of identity not only in the real present, but also in that imaginary nexus where the future and the past create a dialogic lattice of meaning and mystery around my personal sense of selfhood, and where I can wander in the context of whatever oblique sets of moments I may ultimately find myself in "next," or may find myself having been, or will be, or am, or is, or was. . . .

S&S

Get Yourself Decolonized!

From: Sweet & Sour Chicken
Date: June 2, 2006
To: closetchicken listserv

I'm glad Buffalo Chicken has raised the question about the term "decolonized" because I've always wondered myself what it means, and the question comes up for me every time I see it being used. So I went to the bookstore about a year ago and came across a fascinating book published not long ago by Richard Grounds et al. that looked like it might be helpful on the subject, but I'm not entirely sure I understood it correctly. Maybe some of you can help get me straight on this.

In any case, for what it's worth, I came away with the impression that the idea of getting "decolonized" has something to do with empowering your communal health by diligently cleansing yourself of unwanted and dangerous "subaltern" intellectual accumulations. Evidence of having a problem in this area can be manifested in many forms, not the least of which is when you find yourself engaged in the mindless practice of anthropology and archaeology. If you happen to find yourself in that sad condition, decolonization is the most effective remedy.

You see, decolonization seems to be a process by which invading cultures and their harmful lifeways can be identified and usefully purged. It's said to have the most invigorating impact upon the political tracts of those plagued by unhealthy alien cultures because it clears the way for the resurgence of more healthy forms of culture.

Based on my admittedly casual study of the matter, I have the impression that one so "decolonized" will immediately notice a whole new revitalized outlook on life, being guaranteed to discover an empowering capacity for distinguishing at a glance indigenous right-thinkingness from imperialist wrong-thinkingness.

At least, I sense that it is much advised as a process that can aid you with the challenge of getting your racial and ethnic intellectual parts properly cleansed.

I've noticed how proponents of the cleansing process speak of the disease of "colonization" as a problematic historical condition. But typically, these advocates of decolonization are thankfully very thin on boringly complicated historical analysis and seem to prefer being generous with issuing much more fun and readily useful moralizing labels like "sellout."

You may also take note of how those who have been successfully decolonized usually thereafter display an amazing ability to sort things out via racialism and via promotion of ultra-patriotic racialist tribal nationalism and via advocacy for race-based cultural separatism, but once you've gotten yourself decolonized, the benefits are said to be wonderfully efficacious for the overall health of the body politic.

Having been advised by other more knowledgeable cultural health practitioners that I'm long overdue for the process myself, I suggest that everyone in the Coop should look into getting it done right away!

S&S

If Ward Churchill Is Indian, Aren't You Too, Chicken Nuggets?

From: Sweet & Sour Chicken
Date: June 22, 2006
To: closetchicken listserv

Hello biofeathered bantamologists:

As the years go by and I struggle to understand what I mean when I say that race is a challenging problem to solve rather than something to perpetuate, I sense that many of you disagree and plan to go on doing race because it's important to you and to your world, while others have trouble, as I do, with sorting out what it means to challenge the practice of race and to explain what this means. I don't wish to suggest that it's strictly a matter of taking a position; maybe so for some people, but for others maybe it's more a matter of deciding how you feel along the way.

Figuring out what to do about race isn't easy; one might well roam about feeling a little lost, wondering where to go next. Toward this end, I often use the Coop as a place to let my mind wander. It's strange, you know, because so much of my life has been like that, not a journey with convenient destinations, measurable distances, a sequence of named places.

As you know, I've been exploring my sense of self and my notions of race and at times it seems important for me to say to myself that maybe we could change the world, couldn't we? No doubt for most of us, as in my case, changing the world seems less likely than the prospect of wandering about aimlessly and getting mostly lost while looking inside at who we've been, who we are, and who we'll become next. So for this reason, I give myself permission to say something foolish once in a while.

I'm no longer an Indian, that's certain, but maybe I'll always be an Indian in some sense. Realizing this, in my most recent emails I've deliberately brought up race and ethnicity, putting the two terms side-by-side to reflect a realization that I had last year while in the midst of wandering in the land of rangers and bears and Hispanics and inward regions with no names, no maps, no clear destinations.

∾

But while pondering the mysteries of race and ethnicity and wondering whether to say something about that, I started thinking about the treatment Ward Churchill has received at the hands of racial Indians in response to his claims of having Indian ancestry. I've been vaguely weaving in and out of the news about the Churchill situation over the last year and a half—the investigation by the University of Colorado into his record of scholarship and charges of plagiarism and falsification of research.

Some of his critics like Jodi Rave and Suzan Harjo would seemingly prefer that CU focus on Churchill's self-identification as an Indian. I think they are too tough on his lack of bioracial Indian credentials.

I make this observation because I think of race as a cultural behavior. I see race as a cultural construction that would gain clarity and meaning if we detach it from its pseudobiological origins. With this in mind, I would treat race as a form of ethnicity, and I'd argue that we shouldn't treat ethnicity as a form of race.

Moving along this path, this is how I ultimately meander into thinking that the quality of Indianness/Nativeness/Indigenousness should logically be treated as a purely cultural construction. And given Churchill's long exposure to "Indian" culture (whatever "Indian culture" might be in the absence of the now-detached verification of bioracial authority) Churchill surely has gathered more than a few drops of Indian culture in him by now, so wouldn't this make him a bona fide Indian/Native American/Indigenous person?

In fact, maybe we can usefully apply what might be termed "the Churchill test" to sort out people who hold a faith-based belief in race as biology from people who accept the truth about race as pure culture. If you see Churchill as non-Native due to the absence of identifiable Indians in his family tree (to be sure, what is an "Indian" ancestor if race is cultural and not biological?), then you believe in the idea of race as something that is biological, not cultural. If you view Churchill as a legitimate Native American/American Indian/Indian/Indigene on the basis of race-as-culture despite the absence of any identifiable Indian ancestry, then you truly see race as a cultural construction.

I like this test because it tells us what we think. It tells us where we stand on race. With this test in hand, we can see where we are in life when it comes to race.

☙❧

Anyway, all this roaming to & fro suggests another interesting thought. If we find out that we think of race as a product of culture rather than as an outcome of biology, and if we decide to be liberal about it and treat Indian ethnic identity in terms of something like a one drop rule, isn't Chicken Nuggets a legitimate Native American/American Indian/Indian/Native/Indigene?

Hello Chicken Nuggets! Surely you have gathered many drops of Indian culture in yourself by now. Surely you must admit this truth. Wouldn't it be wrong for you to deny the existence in your sense of selfhood the many drops of Indian cultural exposure that have helped to shape who you are? Aren't you an Indian? I'd guess that everyone on this list has at least one or two drops of Indian cultural blood.

Chickens, according to the logic of my wandering mind, would you agree that Chicken Nuggets is an Indian and he should admit it? I presume that most of you are reluctant to come this far with me. Fair enough. I feel doubtful anyway that Chicken Nuggets feels comfortable with this journey and the way I've decided for him that he's an Indian. It's not that I want him to be an Indian, it's just that in some sense he is, and he might as well admit it.

Mulling over the identity of Chicken Nuggets for him, we can usefully question the liberal one-drop cultural standard, of course, and weigh in with ideas about how many cultural drops it takes to be a viable ethnic Indian, black, white, Hispanic, Asian, whatever. I favor the view, for example, that I'm an ethnic black person (based in part on my years of listening to the Rolling Stones and from the fact that I own an Eminem CD), knowing that others may well quibble with my argument.

But the point is that culture does not respect pseudobiology and its Maginot lines drawn in the ever-shifting sands of selfhood. Culture gets inside us whether we want it to or not. Identity and selfhood must necessarily be mysteriously complex artifacts buried deep inside us, because we need adaptable personal resources to aid us in negotiating our way through the many nuanced social situations we face each day. Decisions about identity must reflect that complexity. What do you find when you spend time excavating yourselves in the dark, Chickens? Who are we?

All my wandering aside, from the evidence I've seen in Chicken chatter, race is not particularly complex. It isn't usually treated in the Coop as the kind of purely cultural production that I describe along the road I've followed here. Instead, the constructions of Nativeness and Indianhood seem to be employed most commonly as if race were an inflexible biological reality with clean edges and not a messy matter of pure culture, so it seems fair to say that the doings of Chickenry mostly seem aimed at the destination of enacting and perpetuating race in its traditional biological incarnation.

☉☉

There's a map on the wall of the Coop and we all pause to see how far we must go to bring more Indians into archaeology, and to get white archaeologists more sensitive to partnership, and in the end, to move toward decolonizing non-Native archaeology as a profession. Aren't the Closet

Chickens doing race? Or does it have to do with something that isn't strictly race, like anti-colonial historical analysis?

For those of you who endorse the idea of decolonizing archaeology, the history of race ought to be of some interest as something created in Europe—an ideology that slipped its wandering way across the ocean to become thoroughly domesticated in America as a production of colonialism. The idea of being Indian didn't originate with Indians, though racial Indianhood is heartily espoused by Indians today as if it had been dreamed into our lives by some enlightened Indian philosopher, rather than cooked up by colonialism and Enlightenment science.

Doing race feels like an indigenous thing to do, but race is a cultural import from Europe and its colonies. Given this history, when we enact racial Indianhood, we are clearly embracing the enactment and perpetuation of the legacy of colonialism. I don't mean to attach a moral judgment to such enactments, but proponents of anti-colonialism often do just that, seemingly unaware of the fact that promoting Nativeness without challenging race implies moral acceptance of the legacy of colonialism.

As I see it, the decolonization movement in Indian country has to do mostly with countering "white" power with "Indian" power. Isn't this race at work? Shouldn't "decolonizing archaeology" have something to do with challenging the way race is done in the discipline today? Shouldn't the challenge to colonialism involve a careful rethinking of race? Shouldn't truly committed decolonizers hesitate to promote the idea of being Indian and the notion that there is such a thing as a biologically white archaeologist? Or is it our intention in the Coop, as with the Ward Churchillians, to accept race and to feel good about being Indian and to bond over being Native and non-Native and to simply refer to colonialism as a putative problem while actually being bent on perpetuating it via race? If only race and being Indian were truly and reassuringly biological, and not so confusingly cultural!

It's easy to go along with race, I know. For this reason, I can't imagine that Chickens would ever permit Chicken Nuggets to be the Indian that he is. I can't imagine that Chicken Nuggets himself would ever feel comfortable acting on his all-too-real drops of Indian/Native cultural identity, even though he may well choose to sit down to a breakfast of cornflakes, have lunch with a corndog, feast on roasting ears at dinner, and later a movie with popcorn—all the while saying to himself and to the Coop: "There's nothing Indian about me!"

I sometimes suspect that this is the Coop's true destination: to have a world in which Chicken Nuggets can never explore his Indianness because he lacks the proper pseudo-drops of racial blood. Not that I want him to be an Indian. After all, I'm not an Indian, that's certain, but maybe I'm still an Indian, culturally speaking, and maybe Chicken Nuggets really is an Indian, culturally speaking.

I think it's important to ponder such things because it seems to mean that we can cultivate many marvelously adaptive and integrative ways of being ourselves, but only if we redefine race as ethnicity and only if we reject the idea of treating ethnicity as if it were race. Because race as biology is not only wrong, it is inflexible, immutable, insurmountable, separatist, oppressively colonialistic. Ethnicity, on the other hand—if not tainted and suborned by the warping cruelties of unchallenged racialism—seems self-empowering because it is readily configured to enhance our power to choose who we want to be, to express who we are. We can truly change; we can become many new things; we can wander and get lost inside ourselves once in a while.

Sometimes I feel idealistic and I see how ethnicity explains the character of our Coop. Or does race better explain who we are? I feel afraid sometimes. Whatever hopes or fears I feel about race, it is my suggestion that race should be transformed away from rigid pseudobiology and toward elastic cultural ethnicity.

☙❧

Chickens, you may take seriously or take lightly my characterization of Chicken Nuggets as an ethnic Indian, but postponing careful consideration of race will not keep change at bay.

Anyway, whatever the future holds or does not hold as I wander in and out of the Coop, I know I have little to offer in the way of any particular destination. For now, I'm content with a more self-centered exploration of who I've been, who I am, who I might become next. So I plan to keep wandering, changing into the person I really am.

And, to be sure, I do presume that if we wish, we really can change the whole world along the way. At least, I give myself permission to say foolish things like that once in a while.

S&S

Gameplay

From: Sweet & Sour Chicken
Date: August 23, 2006
To: closetchicken listserv

Electrochicken Technocoopsters,

This morning I awoke from a dream in which I visited the University of Colorado anthropology building, walking up the main interior staircase. It seemed darker than I recall, and when I placed a hand in one corner, it came away entangled with cobwebs.

I was looking in the dream for the way upstairs. To get to the floor where the graduate seminars are held, one must be sufficiently initiated into the mysteries of CU anthroacademia to have learned the secret passageways that spiral up to the hidden final floor of the building. But for some reason, I was stuck on the main staircase.

Waking, I thought it a propitious time to read Prairie Chicken's "The Technomechanics of Plains Indian Coiled Gambling Baskets," which appeared in my mailbox the other day within the latest issue of *Plains Anthropologist*. I went outside to what my wife and I call our Stargazer Bench to read it. I don't often read technical papers word-for-word; I tend to skim such things until I find something that I really want to know. Then I backtrack as needed to get the point.

This time I read the whole paper and I enjoyed reading it. I liked Prairie Chicken's tone and skillful use of language and confident deployment of technical terminology. It's a knowledgeable and profusely illustrated paper.

I don't want to suggest that readers should overlook the uncritical deployment of race. This is a paper that believes in race, and it appears in an anthropology journal that also believes in race. But to benefit from scholarly research pertaining to the ancient Pawnee homeland, I must set aside the distraction of seeing race deployed as an academic prerequisite.

Anyway, I was most interested in Prairie Chicken's speculative suggestions regarding the possible history that might account for the spread of "the Plains Indian coiled basket technological complex." It reminds me that someday I'd like to get back into the study of ancient history (I don't like the term "prehistory" and the unscholarly assumptions that empower this term—assumptions that devalue oral documents). Maybe I'll go back in time to ancient Pawneeland again when I've gotten bored with defeating race and getting defeated by it.

Some of Prairie Chicken's ideas echo my own assessment of Caddoan and Siouan oral traditions regarding population movements, agriculture, and women's social history in ancient America. I wrote some stuff on this when I was in grad school at CU, back when they let me wander unsupervised to discover some of the secrets of the CU anthro building. This was also the topic of the paper I gave at the 2001 Dartmouth symposium that launched the Coop.

I hope Prairie Chicken continues his research. It deserves longer treatment.

☉☉

Another thought comes to mind as I consider the topic of gambling baskets. Last month I found myself in Pawnee, Oklahoma, and one humid evening my sister took me across town to visit the Pawnee Nation casino. Gas pumps sat in front of it, and there was a parking lot full of cars. When I stepped inside, the room glowed with cheerful electronica. My sister chose a hulking glassy marvel of superchipped technogamery while I wandered around studying all the other hopeful gamblers in their seats.

In contrast to the basket and dice game, it looks like lonely work sitting in the Pawnee casino feeding paper money into the hungry slots, pressing the magic buttons with palm or finger, depending on which technique feels luckiest. The room has a lively tone, but people don't seem like they'd appreciate it if you tried to strike up a conversation, although the woman seated next to my sister was very friendly—and very lucky.

I tried my hand modestly, sitting down on the other side of my sister and feeding a dollar-bill into a futuristic gothic-horror Aliens-themed machine, like a pilot at the controls of a doomed spaceship. My sister helped me to set the controls for the heart of the sun and I blasted off. My first press of the magic button gave up a rewarding whizzbang and the machine displayed an inviting row of alien eggs, which I pressed one-by-one until a facehugger with acid for blood leaped forth to end my lucky streak. Deciding to jump ship in my escape-pod with my modest winnings, I quit and came away 56 cents wealthier.

☉☉

Pawnee women today do not gamble with woven baskets and dice as they once did—as their ancestors did, long ago. Studying the technology involved, Prairie Chicken gives us a marvelous glimpse of ancient hands at work in the distant past. Indian hands, he terms them. I argue that most of these hands were the hands of people who weren't involved in the historical culture of race, so those folk were not adherents to racial Indian identity. The dictates of racialism require that they be called Indians anyway.

Prairie Chicken's acceptance of this racial logic has much good company in anthropology. Skimming the other ten papers and book reviews in that same issue of *Plains Anthropologist* (volume 51, # 197, 2006), I count 72 references to the structures of race, with mention of "Indians," "Natives," and "Paleoindians." A few of these referents may arguably be appropriate, referring, as they do, to practitioners of racial Indianhood. But other usages flow from long-established conventions that deserve thoughtful recalibration, and a number of these terms of race are plainly impossible to justify.

In an otherwise fascinating paper by James Keyser, Linea Sundstrom, and George Poetschat, for example, these coauthors feel free to declare that certain topics in ancient rock art reflect "an important part of northern Plains Indian religion during the Late Prehistoric Period[.]" But since there were no adherents to racial Indianhood anywhere in America during that time period, there simply couldn't have been anything that could usefully be termed an "Indian" religion.

Interestingly, two of the papers and one book review somehow manage to proceed without racial references. This suggests to me that it might very well be possible to forgo the heavy reliance on racial taxonomy that too often festers at the heart of twenty-first century anthropology. I'm not sure why this seems like such a revolutionary suggestion, but it is.

For Prairie Chicken's paper, he incorporates several photos of a family heirloom gambling basket. It is very touching to imagine how this research must have felt to him—the meaningful sense of connection to ancestors who took pleasure in the basket and dice game. But most of those many generations of his ancestors cannot be properly termed "Indians." Using anthropological scholarship to delve into the ancient doings of those people, modern anthropology has at least one obvious lesson to learn about respecting the actual truths of their lives.

S&S

The Saga of "Kee-wuch-oo-ta-kaa"

From: Sweet & Sour Chicken
Date: September 23, 2006
To: closetchicken listserv

Chicken Noodle, I have a response to your recent inquiry to the Coop. In years past, I've gotten involved in several instances of repatriations involving non-skeletal soft tissue, mostly scalps. One situation in particular might be of interest to you. It's a troubling story and it saddens me to think of it.

In May 1994 the US embassy in Sweden contacted me about some remains held by the Karolinska Institute in Stockholm. They had skin from the upper torso and head of a man said to have been Pawnee. The embassy official read me the man's name as it had been transcribed, and I immediately confirmed the name as Pawnee, translated as White Fox. The embassy facilitated contact with a researcher in Sweden and I learned the awful details.

Three Skidi Pawnees traveled to Sweden in late 1874 and White Fox fell ill with tuberculosis in Gothamburg and died in early 1875. Citing Swedish anatomy law of the time, Swedish authorities refused to permit his two companions (who were two brothers from a prominent Skidi family) to take White Fox's body back to America with them. Instead, the Institute of Anatomy at the Karolinska Institute decided to prepare a plaster cast of the upper body and head of White Fox, and they pulled his skin over it. They put White Fox on display at Sweden's first anthropological exhibition in 1878.

When I picture this scene, it's difficult to look at him.

I look because I think White Fox has something important to say to us all. So in the years since then, I've paused occasionally to listen. I want to learn something useful out of this. Even so, I don't get it. What worthwhile knowledge did we accrue from this treatment of White Fox? I listen, but I can't hear much beyond my horror.

It might well be convenient for some to blame "white people" for this outrage. But placing generalized culpability on adherents to racial whiteness for this awful situation isn't particularly helpful, so that's not my path. We must lay the blame directly on the Karolinska Institute and their Swedish masters.

They deserve for the world to remember forever what they did to White Fox. People will readily get the meaning of it; the horror.

⊙⊙

I've been hearing lately that some nice people are writing a book about White Fox. Several of my relatives have tried to get me to talk to them. I've found that I can't bring myself to do it. These nice researchers have wisely convinced the Pawnee Nation to support their project. And I have the impression that their research may involve a genetic testing procedure of some kind.

I don't know what they have in mind. In general I'm supportive of scientific inquiry. Will we learn something useful? I hope so.

But in this case I feel suspicious. I wonder if their plan has something to do with genetic testing that promises to identify one's "Indian" ancestry. Send in a swab and find out if you're Indian! This type of testing exploits what little we know of the human genetic map by exaggerating somewhat vague statistical possibilities into definitive pseudoscientific probabilities. People are most readily taken in by such procedures when they believe in race, when they accept the unjustified notion that race is genetic.

To be sure, my suspicions might prove unwarranted. Maybe I'll read that book someday and I'll learn something useful and I'll say, sure, okay, I get it now.

☉☉

Anyway, back in 1994 I had an emotionally difficult job to do and I did some research and I wrote a short paper for the Pawnee Nation on the sad strange saga of White Fox. I found information indicating that he'd probably been a veteran of the Pawnee Scouts.

Hearing the story, all the Pawnees felt stunned and wanted to see him come home. So I prepared some correspondence for the Pawnee Nation to send to the relevant Swedish authorities and they organized the return of his remains for proper burial in Oklahoma in January 1996.

Kiwaku Taka was a young man when he discovered Sweden, when he fell ill among the Swedes, when he died in their distant, terrifying land.

At White Fox's burial, two Skidi singers—my cousins Tom Knife Chief and Steve Knife Chief—honored him with a song that is sung every year during the Pawnee Memorial Day Dance: the Pawnee Scout honor song. If you ever hear this song at this dance, it is slow and somber and beautifully moving in a mysterious way. Everyone listens quietly.

Picturing this scene, I think all the Pawnees hear something meaningful and unfathomable in that song. But for me it's slow and somber and beautifully moving in a mysterious way.

Maybe someday I'll understand the mystery. I'll listen and it'll suddenly come to me. I'll figure out what it means, and I'll say, okay, I finally get it.

Yes, I get it now.

S&S

Deep Time, Chicken Freeko

From: Sweet & Sour Chicken
Date: February 8, 2007
To: closetchicken listserv

Fourteen months ago in December 2005, in the course of contributing to our discussions about Vine Deloria, Chicken Freeko raised an important question that I've been thinking about lately. He wondered why it is deemed necessary by most scholars to rely on science to assess oral traditions.

This is a topic that adherents to racial Indianhood often raise as a way to deploy racial allegiances, as a way to sort people into Indians and their anti-Indian oppressors. Some scholars also use the subject in a similar fashion, but here the intention is to sort out scholars from their anti-science oppressors.

These extremes offer entertainingly attractive options for many scholars and race-practitioners—denoting, no doubt, a casual investment at best in the study of oral traditions. For the rest of us, these options are not particularly satisfying.

In the work of Adrienne Mayor, she tells us why fossils and traditional knowledge have interesting things to say about each other. She constructs a sophisticated argument in favor of the usefulness of subjecting oral documents to analytical dissection, arguing that oral documents about ancient times must be taken seriously in academic scholarship, but researchers should be cautious when it comes to blanket claims of literal historicity.

Mayor's approach to oral traditions can be usefully contrasted to that taken by Bird Man in *Archaeology of the Soul* and other writings. Bird Man analyzes oral documents for insights into the evolution of cultural connections and the transmission of cultural ideas, opening fascinating vistas into deep time. Mayor's analysis, however, doesn't necessarily imply that the information she studies in oral records took shape in the ancient past. Her analytical strategy refrains from inquiring into the durability and antiquity of orally transmitted information.

These two approaches to the study of oral records do not necessarily have an oppositional relationship, but they do stand apart from my approach, which is to hunt for information in the oral record that arguably preserves firsthand glimpses of antiquity. My approach, as in the case of Mayor and Bird Man, assumes that scholarly analysis provides an ideologically appropriate basis for the study of verbal literature.

A fourth approach is to treat oral documents as inerrant historical texts that may occasionally draw in a very selective way upon science and academic scholarship. This is the approach preferred by Vine Deloria in *Red Earth, White Lies*, where he relegates scientific scholarship to an optional support role. I presume Deloria would argue that, in contrast to the academically oriented approaches favored by me, Mayor, and Bird Man, his approach to oral tradition is more ideologically compatible with an assertive allegiance to the tenets of racial Indianhood.

A fifth approach is to argue that oral information does not shed any useful light on antiquity. This is the perspective that was argued in the Kennewick Man case by eight prominent American anthropologists and their academic supporters. And as you know, this is the viewpoint that was ultimately adopted by the court. I presume that the plaintiff-scholars and their supporters would favor the view that this treatment of oral tradition is most compatible with an assertive allegiance to the tenets of academic scholarship.

Studying the papers filed before the court, however, I noticed that the Kennewick plaintiffs and their supporters refrained entirely from any mention whatsoever of the work done by me, Mayor, Bird Man, and others who believe that scholarship ought to take seriously the study of oral traditions. This strategy of rejecting oral traditions while keeping silent about the diversity of scholarly routes of inquiry seemingly intends to hold at bay anti-science religionism and governmental bureaucracies. But it does so by ignoring scholarly research.

The ideology of scholarship, it seems to me, devolves into biased partisanship when it ignores scholarship that is inconvenient. It troubles me when I think that the highly respected Kennewick plaintiff-scholars and their allies have taken this path—and it disappoints me when I suspect that the vast majority of their colleagues in academia will defer to their leadership rather than hold them accountable. It also troubles me when adherents to racial Indianhood advise us to ignore scholarship that is inconvenient, and when this advice is rendered for the purpose of promoting racial bonding.

I take it for granted that in terms of ideological identity, we Chickens can encourage one another to be free and to take wing wherever we might choose. But in the end, I trust that members of the Coop will prefer to aim at conscientiously sorting out biased partisanship from useful scholarship.

S&S

I Find Wisdom in the Fringes

From: Sweet & Sour Chicken
Date: January 5, 2008
To: closetchicken listserv

This last December I decided I'd take a break from doing the things I usually do. And in the midst of doing the unusual alternative to the usual things I do, I took a break from taking a break to visit Steve Holen and Chip Colwell-Chanthaphonh at the Denver Museum of Nature and Science.

Steve has told me about his research on mammoth bones over the years, and I took this as a chance to get caught up. His research has borne some unusual results, providing evidence for a pre-Clovis human occupation of the central plains. It seems that since I last spoke with him on this topic some years ago, he's made some encouraging progress in chipping away at the skepticism of his colleagues.

He showed me a little temporary DMNS exhibit on his research. It turned out to be situated—appropriately enough—a bit off the beaten track. His ideas are not mainstream ideas in archaeology for now. His analytical techniques, however, fit very well into what mainstream archaeologists do. In any case, I thought the tone of the exhibit was a bit too cautious. And a little confusing. Rather than putting forward a definitive argument and then letting critics speak for themselves, the voice of the exhibit seemed to say: *This idea of Steve's is interesting, sure, but it only deserves a very hesitantly cautious maybe.*

I stood there and realized that I have no idea what it takes to win people over when you have an idea that qualifies as unusual. Peering at a hugely assertive mammoth bone at the bottom of the exhibit, I wondered how declarative assertiveness compares to a tone of quietly argued academic caution in terms of the end result: winning peer support.

I felt very pleased to meet Chip. I liked his gentle confidence. A good person to hang out with. A very lively conversation ensued among the three of us. In the midst of taking time out from doing what I do, I'm glad I took time out to drive down to Denver that day. And Chip gave me his new book, co-edited with Egg White: *Collaboration in Archaeological Practice: Engaging Descendant Communities.* I note that various Chickens appear therein. Chicken Noodle, Chicken à la Queen, and Chicken Nuggets. A group of very interesting writings, for sure.

Thanks, Chip.

☜☞

I was particularly intrigued with the paper written by Chicken Nuggets: "Unusual or 'Extreme' Beliefs about the Past, Community Identity, and Dealing with the Fringe." I read it in detail because I often sense that when I do what I do, I usually stand at the edge of things, somewhere out on the unusual fringes.

Nuggets proposes at the outset to give some useful guidance to archaeologists on how they should "respond when people don't believe them[.]" But I'm less interested in the problems of academic archaeologists than I am in the possibility of extracting a few insightful principles that might apply to my particular situation.

What do you do when people don't go along with what you do?

I like the way Chicken Nuggets provides essential and enlightening explication of such terms as "hypothesis" and "theory" and "truth" and "validity." Even so, I find it hard to go along with some statements, like when he says: "[W]hat non-scientists often believe can be true, but not necessarily valid." Nuggets attempts to do more here than engage in a bit of terminological lawyering, but this is nevertheless where he loses me. My skepticism kicks in. And here I'm going to be blunt. My skepticism unfortunately takes the popular form of "I-don't-go-along-with-this-bullshit" rather than the academic "I-will-now-deploy-a-questioning-attitude-as-a-useful-analytical-tool."

It's not very flattering for me that I respond so strongly to Nuggets' thoughtful reasoning, but this is the hurdle his argument suddenly must now cross. I read on. It's fascinating, the tale that follows.

But before we get there, I'm stumbling again. This time over "dominant society" versus "American Indians and other Indigenous peoples[.]" I feel suspicious. Is this a race-based analysis? If I'm right, isn't it a problem of some kind?

Those of us who question race—scholars like me and Chicken Nuggets—we must struggle constantly with the power that race wields and its humbling ability to shape how we talk. It seems common for Chickens in general to deploy an analysis that sounds like historical process (relying on terms like "indigenous" and "colonial"), and maybe people can be counted on to read it that way, as if such terms imply a non-racial analysis.

As I see it (to borrow from some of Nuggets' observations), this way of doing race is an "intuitive science" approach that hopes for the "brute fact" of racial cultural practice to obscure the fact that one is doing bioracial analysis, not historical process. I suspect that if you deploy these terms according to an analysis that really does invoke historical process, it doesn't look like race anymore. And I suspect that what Nuggets does at this point in his essay is to reference a truly invalid racial analysis that merely poses as historical process. Race is the hugely assertive mammoth bone that begs notice at the bottom of his terminology.

Anyway, Nuggets' paper doesn't dwell on this point. This particular giant bone proves to be a minor distraction, important only to fringe analyst types like me. And to be sure, I'm often enough guilty of committing the very same unnatural offense against nature. Race is a convenient truth, even if an invalid one.

☙

So Nuggets moves on to relate a fascinating story that implies a model of ancient history that mainstream archaeology does not accept, for the most part. And this also happens to be a model that plays havoc with the 1492 boundary that is commonly summoned forth to reify racial analytical discourse (red indigenes versus white colonialists). But not to worry, Nuggets suggests that in the absence of a transparent peer review process, this threatening construction of the past ought not to be accepted as a valid treatment of the evidence. I'm with him on this point. He's won my heart here. Science is not democratic in its processes.

But… but scholarship is very democratic in what it chooses to do as a matter of practice. I think here of Indian Studies. Indian Studies doesn't study the culture of adherents to racial Indianhood. No. It studies Indians! It doesn't matter that the Indian Studies bioracial discursive approach is invalid from a scientific standpoint. It matters more what scholars do democratically.

In this particular world, in Indianstudiesland, Indian people are a biological racial group. Period. This assumption serves as the coin of this particular realm, so to hell with what science says about race being a cultural idea, not a biological reality. We'll do bioracialism anyway. Maybe we won't call it "race" anymore. Sure. We'll say "indigenous" and "colonialism" and we'll deny that race is doing the heavy lifting. Deferring to race as a "brute fact," we just can't be bothered with any fringe experimental discourse that really treats race as culture, not biology.

☙

It's interesting to know that the "weird belief" in our racial world is mine. For I believe in confronting race. And in terms of the fateful determination of adherents to racial Indianhood to just go on doing race no matter what, I don't fit in. I reject what Nuggets mentions as the "received wisdom"—that is, concerning how to talk in a scholarly way about the doings of humankind, knowing what we know about race.

Embracing the practice of racial identity in America, racialists dominate the dominant society. And race is in charge of the academy. In the total absence of an explicit non-racial cultural option, academic racialists and their general public of supportive committed adherents to race oppress my tiny non-racial community every day with the "brute fact" of their brutally dominant culture.

Brutally Dominant Racialist Indian Studies Academic Chickens: if you want to get along with me and my unpopular "extreme" anti-race fringe community, you must follow very carefully what Nuggets has to say about how to deal with fringe-types. I see that now.

Toward that end (doing a bit of creative rephrasing here), Nuggets implies that racialist academics "do not need to believe" what I relate about myself and my anti-race ideological system, and it would do little or no good "to *challenge* or *deny*" the story I tell. You would "do better to allow for… a wider range of views[,]" like the ones I espouse. And "[r]ather than say that [you have] *the* truth… [you] might be better off saying that [you] have *a* truth." And to challenge my fringe anti-race beliefs "carries risks." To respond to me "too strongly is probably going to reinforce [my fringe anti-race] beliefs—not change them." Finally, there is power in what you Brutally Dominant Racialists do, but when you do it, it must be done with a sense of "respect and humility."

☉☉

All this seems very wise to me. And saddening. I'm not particularly fond of living on the fringe of things, easily dismissed. But I willingly visit the Coop as it is, not as I might wish it to be, so I'm glad I took the time to read this paper with its sad wisdom. I like the idea of people finding ways to get along despite their highly polarized viewpoints.

Thank you, Chicken Nuggets.

For sure, all of you Brutally Dominant Racialist Indian Studies Academic Chickens should give careful thought as to how to deal with oppressed fringe folk like me. If I sound a little too blunt at times, you must remember that I have a very real social justice bone to pick with you and your continuing oppression of me and my tiny fringe anti-race community. As long as the academy sees no need to create a non-racial cultural option for visitors like me, I must scurry warily beneath the relentless mammoth tread of race.

Doing race, Chickens, you wield the awesome implacable colonialistic power of your dominant social paradigm. Your practice of race is uncaring in its willingness to suppress my truth, in its harshly casual tyranny of my unusual little validities.

In this hypothesis, I try to invalidate all my hesitantly cautious maybes, the logical outcomes of my weirdly fantastic truths. I try to look into the future beyond the accumulated details to the end results, but even though the view is extreme, I can't see very far.

Standing here in the fringes beyond the door of the Coop, I hypothesize that race is the giant bone that sinks slowly into the ground between us. It whispers spirally fractured colossal truths, assertively vain validities. Its quiet academic arguments sound hugely declarative to me, even if I can't figure out the difference between winning and losing.

In any case, December 2007 has come and gone, and now it is another year, and I'm glad I took a little holiday from doing the unusual things I usually do.

S&S

If Anyone Asks

From: Sweet & Sour Chicken
Date: April 22, 2008
To: closetchicken listserv

Indigenologists,

Sometimes I think I know a lot of things—sometimes I might even be a little wise. But just as often I feel like I wouldn't know what to say if anyone asked. Like, occasionally it bothers me that I don't have an unambiguous sense for what is meant by "indigenous archaeology."

It wasn't always this way. Chicken Nuggets' recent reminiscences to the Coop on his involvement with what is known now as "indigenous archaeology" got me thinking about the late 1980s, circa 1990.

I remember how disappointed I felt when the Pawnee Tribe and the Native American Rights Fund asked Waldo Wedel for help. He lived right there in Boulder, Colorado, and he said no, he wouldn't help the Pawnees try to figure out what the archaeological evidence said about Pawnee ancestors.

Nuggets immediately agreed to help us. *Yeah, sure I'll help*, he said to me when I asked. No worry. I had expected to stand there in South Dakota and give him a sales pitch about how I thought it important to try to put oral traditions together with archaeological evidence, and maybe we could together figure out how to use oral traditions as historical documents, how to respect the archaeological record. A way to understand ancient history.

Let me tell you, it was quite a relief to meet Chicken Nuggets and to have him come to Boulder and work with us, and to try to put things together. I stood there at the Native American Rights Fund thinking to myself, *So this is what it's like to work with an archaeologist, rather than sit across from them, all of them sitting there wishing you'd get up and go away.*

I respected Nuggets. His wisdom, humility; his quiet way of knowing. And it was nice how he treated me like a colleague even though I felt like I didn't really know very much just yet. I was trying to learn about oral traditions and archaeology, trying to get myself into a place where I'd have something to say about what I knew if anyone asked. Chicken Nuggets asked. Those other archaeologists in those days, they wouldn't talk to me; they wouldn't ask. Not even Waldo Wedel.

In 1991, after Wedel refused to help us, I sent him a publication by me and Nuggets: archaeology/oral traditions; the path to—as I saw it then, seeing it in racial terms—ancient Indian history. I sent it to Wedel with a note: *I just thought you might enjoy reading this; no need to write back—Roger Echo-Hawk.* And sure enough, he didn't write back.

Then in May 1992 I happened to meet Wedel in Boulder. A tall, kindly man. Still feeling very much an outsider, I had snuck into the auditorium to listen to a talk by Dennis Stanford. Was I their enemy in those days?

After the talk, I saw the old man standing in the hall with his wife, Mildred. I walked over. No one introduced us. I had slipped into the hall to listen to Dennis Stanford talk and then … it was like I had snuck up on him, the old man, Waldo Wedel. I said my name and we shook hands. I could see that he knew who I was. A brief little smile lit his eyes. Maybe he felt a little embarrassed, but not really.

I said, "I've admired your work over the years, and I've learned a lot from what you've done." This must have been something he had heard often enough over the years. This time he nodded and paused a moment.

"Well, there are some things I wish I had done differently."

I think I knew what he meant. He hadn't helped the Pawnees because he didn't like the controversy around reburial. Reburial was deemed in his world to be an anti-science thing to do. Maybe he bore us no ill will, the Pawnee

Tribe, but in the end he had refused to help us. Now hearing my compliment, perhaps he knew what I meant.

And it couldn't be helped, the way I necessarily came across at that moment as the spokesperson for the whole Pawnee Tribe. I decided I'd give him a gift, the old man. Goodwill should never be deemed too precious to give away for free.

Understanding what I had chosen to do, Wedel wanted to say something more meaningful than an amiable thank you. But the moment ended. If it was an awkward moment for him, I couldn't tell. Dennis Stanford and several other people came up to us. I turned to leave. They were all headed for dinner. There would be collegial colleagueship over dinner that night in Boulder.

After Waldo Wedel died in 1996, David Gradwohl wrote a nice obit in *Plains Anthropologist*. It was all about how generous Wedel had been to him, a young student of archaeology. Wedel had written back to him, encouraging him, helping him.

I felt a little sad reading that. Not just personally, but because in the course of Waldo Wedel's long and distinguished career, the Pawnees had asked for his help only once and he'd said no.

Did he deserve even a token gesture of goodwill from us? Maybe not. For sure, he hadn't treated me like a worthwhile colleague. Yet… yet I have always appreciated Wedel's scholarship—I find it worthwhile as a general matter.

But in the end, Waldo Wedel had felt free to dig up some of my ancestors without asking us, and we had felt free to rebury them without asking him. Given this history, I didn't really mind his dismissal of my deep thoughts on ancient history.

Chicken Nuggets gave me something positive and uncomplicated to think about. A gift; an offering of wisdom… the idea that Indians and archaeologists could work together. Yes, I was an Indian then. When I was an Indian I would have known how to define indigenous archaeology.

Looking back to that time, I don't always feel certain about what happened and what it means. If I felt more certain of my certainties, maybe I'd know how to define "indigenous archaeology." Maybe I'd know what to say, if anyone asks.

S&S

The Coop Gets Blumenbached and Neverminded

In late 2004 I launched a series of dialogic introspections with "Kennewick-man," a traveler in imaginary time who lived and died long ago without race, and who got resurrected into our racial world in 1996. A version of that first dialogue appeared in a 2008 book, Kennewick Man: Perspectives on the Ancient One, *edited by Heather Burke and four Closet Chickens. Knowing this book would be read by some leading adherents to racial Indianhood, I continued my efforts to spill the well-kept secret of racialism: that race has problems and needs useful rethinking.*

In 2008 I prepared a sequel for The SAA Archaeological Record. *I designed this second Kennewickman dialogue as a means of drawing the broader archaeo-community into a conversation on race, and to hopefully disturb their professional complacency on the topic.*

For the third interior narrative in this trilogy I turned back to the Coop in late July 2009, sending them the Kennewickman dialogue which follows. I also cc'ed an archaeologist mentioned in this piece, David Meltzer, and he very generously expressed the hope of someday having his own chat with S&S and Kennewickman.

This third dialogue starts where the second dialogue finishes, with Ken-newickman having surrendered to racial identity. In the course of so doing—and in accordance with the rules of race—he has just forced racial identity upon me as well. It's quite a scream and I say:

From: Sweet & Sour Chicken
Date: July 30, 2009
To: closetchicken listserv

S&S: Now that I'm back in the racialist fold with a spike right through my head, Kennewickman, what race am I this time?

KM: As a denizen of the Coop, S&S, you're a featherskinned Closet Chicken. But in terms of race, this time you're a could-have-been alternative to the current racial taxonomy. You're an almost-was. So S&S: now you're an almost half-human semi-beast, an almost *Homo monboddo*. Do you mind?

S&S: I'm pleased to be a Closet Chicken, of course. But a Monboddo? Did you just make that up, Kennewickman? I enjoy hearing your tales of traveling in imaginary time, your origin stories and oral traditions, but you can't just make stuff up. There's no such thing as a *Homo monboddo*.

KM: The thing about race, S&S, is that it is made-up. Racialists don't mind inventing a fake racial past, and when I hear them talk as if race has a history, when I hear them using racial terms to describe people who lived before the invention of race, I think of Lord Monboddo. In the late eighteenth century Lord Monboddo appeared as a transitional figure, living in a world imbued with an ideology that Gottfried Leibniz articulated so well, speaking in 1671 of pre-racial "barbarians": "What a lovely bunch of semi-beasts!" We needed Johann Blumenbach to give us something better. He gave us race.

S&S: That's interesting, Kennewickman. In my rejection of race, I guess I'd still have to admit that it's an improvement over what could have been! But didn't Blumenbach use a bunch of skulls to make up race?

KM: Blumenbach had a collection of skulls and he studied them. But not just to devise racial categories; he relied on those skulls to help him sort out the relationship of humans to other primates, to inquire about our biological family tree.

S&S: So he needed those skulls to investigate who we are, we humans. What if he had dug up your mother's skull, Kennewickman, would you approve of that?

KM: S&S, it wouldn't be easy to find anyone who'd be happy to learn that their parents had been dug up for scientific study. Blumenbach did his best with what he had, but maybe we can try to do better.

S&S: I see what you mean, Kennewickman. I just thought it ironic to picture the invention of racial Indianhood via the study of a collection of skulls by a European scholar, and how it's a fundamental tenet of racial Indianhood today to raise moral and ethical objections to skeletal collections. *C'mon all you Monboddo half-human semi-beasts, let's dig up some skulls and invent race and then we'll rebury all those skulls and we'll defend the doing of racial Indianhood to the death!*

KM: Sure, S&S. The scholarly foundation of the invention of racial Indianhood happened via the study of skulls. I don't know what adherents to racial Indianhood think about this history, but some of them probably don't mind. And I understand, I think. If racial Indianhood is deemed a good thing among adherents to racialism, well, maybe it's because we can sometimes separate the products of knowledge from the production of knowledge.

S&S: So Blumenbach did things that we might view with approval, even if we have some objections to his methods. Should we approve of race, Kennewickman?

KM: I don't know, S&S. That's a useful question, but maybe it's not quite the right question. Practitioners of racial identity almost always feel pretty good about what they are doing. They like race and enjoy doing it. If it gives them pleasure, is that so bad? I don't know. But I do know that when we list the things we don't like about race, it's a pretty impressive list. And people who do race often do it by objecting to the way other people do race. If there were options. . . . If people someday discovered that doing race ought to involve making a choice. . . . With alternatives to racialism ready to hand, maybe people could make more sophisticated judgments and decisions about identity.

S&S: I don't know about that, Kennewickman. Racialism is so entrenched in the world. . . .

KM: Well, one thing seems clear, S&S. I think even you would vote for race rather than for what the predecessors of Lord Monboddo stood for. If the intellectual forebears of Lord Monboddo had gotten their way, S&S, you'd be—

S&S: Oh, I see! Right here. Historian Ivan Hannaford writes on page 210 of his book, *Race: The History of an Idea in the West:* "Blumenbach wrote at a time when Negroes and Native Americans were considered half-animals. . . ."

KM: Just think, S&S, if pre-racial intellectual ideology had prevailed instead of race, adherents to racial Indianhood would all be hurrying around shoring up the idea of being semi-beast half-humans instead of rushing around preserving racial Indianhood. So when they say to one another, "Hey, let's all be Indians," you should say to yourself —

S&S: Thank you, Blumenbach! Gosh, Kennewickman, I wonder what those racial Indians will think to discover that racial Indianhood is really a European thing.

KM: That's not likely to come up, S&S, just hanging out with American archaeologists. See, they like race and they do it all the time and they prefer not to question it.

S&S: I guess you're right, Kennewickman. The other day I went to the bookstore and I picked up David Meltzer's new old book, *First Peoples in a New World.* One encounters racially constructed "Native Americans," "American Indians," and "Paleoindians" almost thirty times before arriving at "Just what do crania tell us about 'race'—whatever that loaded term implies?"

KM: So Meltzer actually says "loaded term. . . ." Hmm. Even so, S&S, it seems that the tenets of race and racial Indianhood persuade him to load up his book with plenty of contemporary presentist pseudoscientific racial assumptions. He loads his book up with a lot of racial Indians!

S&S: Thank you, Johann Blumenbach! If Lord Monboddo and his pre-racial predecessors had prevailed, Meltzer would be talking about Paleohalfhumans and Paleosemibeasts rather than Paleoindians. "O Lord Monboddo," says the hidden text under Meltzer's words: "let there be Indians instead of half-humans; let Indians, not semi-beasts, people my new world!"

KM: That's right, S&S. Meltzer does race as if race tells the truth about human biological diversity, as if there really were "Indians" in ancient America. Some elements of racial identity began to appear maybe as early as the sixteenth century, but race as we know it wasn't invented until the late eighteenth century. I'm not sure why so many scholars ignore this history.

S&S: It's shocking, Kennewickman. Because Meltzer knows the truth! On page 181 he quotes a colleague who knows better—anthropologist Jonathan Marks: "Today the anthropological community en masse rejects as pseudoscientific the notion of race as a natural category. . . ." Weird, huh!? That Meltzer knows this truth and yet—

KM: It's confusing, S&S. I know. It is difficult to understand why people like Meltzer can hear the truth and not listen. And it's no use to just single him out. He's got a lot of company, as you well know, S&S. He just does what all his colleagues do.

S&S: You're talking about oral documents and origin stories, aren't you, Kennewickman. Meltzer chooses to "omit discussion" of oral traditions because his "expertise lies elsewhere." Meltzer brushes off my particular expertise into an endnote and pretty soon we find him diligently boning up on mtDNA expertisery!

KM: Well, S&S, when archaeologists get together, they urge one another to feel afraid of oral traditions. They don't trust that particular brand of expertise since they don't want to get accused of having a whole buncha lotta jumpin' jack flash in their writings. They do their best to aim at being Serious Science-like Scholars. With plenty of all the really good expertisery.

S&S: I get it, Kennewickman. That's understandable. As far as I know, it's not much of an exaggeration to say that the study of the oral transmission of historical knowledge from deep time is pretty much limited to a couple of featherskinned *Homo monboddo* half-human semi-beast Closet Chickens. There is no well-established field of study for ancient American history. Everyone does Paleoindian prehistory. I guess this situation isn't Meltzer's fault, even though he seems unshakably complacent about it. Still, I feel distressed. And I just can't figure out how their Serious Scholarship is really so Serious with stuff like race in it—isn't race a whole lotta buncha jumpin' jack flash?

KM: Sure, S&S. But they've all been jumpin' with all that jack flash for so long it looks like the right kind of expertisery, a Whole Buncha Lotta Very Serious Jumpin' Jack Flash. Race. Even so, it isn't just the fact that the study of deep time oral tradition is such a shallow field of study. Oral tradition just happens to be, well, a little too racial!

S&S: That doesn't make sense, Kennewickman.

KM: Let me clue you in, S&S. You're an Indian to them. A racial Indian.

S&S: Thank you, Johann Blumenbach!

KM: So when you do oral traditions, S&S, to them you do Indian oral traditions. You're being a loyal Indian in their eyes when you talk about oral traditions. Because when they look at you they don't see S&S. They think they see Native Roger Indigenous Echo Indian Hawk, Loyal Aborigine!

S&S: Now I get it, Kennewickman. Sure. Just about where Meltzer stuffs me into an endnote, he says he recognizes that "Native American views of their origins are not always consonant with those of archaeology." So I got consonanted away into racial Indianhood.

KM: You got nativeamericaned into an endnote! Meltzer likes race plenty. But "Indian" oral traditions… well, that's just not his bag, even though he's willing enough to tote quite a lot of other bags in his book. It's a loyalty thing, S&S. An identity thing. He's David I'm-Not-An-Indian Meltzer; he's David I'm-A-Serious-Scholar-Of-Serious-Science-Like-Archaeology Meltzer. You're just an Indian to him. Always will be. End of story: you've been dismissed from anthropology and sent off to Indian Studies!

S&S: But he knows the truth about race, Kennewickman. He knows! Maybe if I wrote to him and tried to —

KM: What? Tried to tell him the truth about race? C'mon, S&S! Don't be such a half-human semi-beast! He already knows the truth and he doesn't care. For his third edition he'd just look for another endnote to reservation you into.

S&S: But maybe if I sent him a Serious Science-Like email he'd listen! I'm sure of it. It would happen like this: Meltzer would read it and he'd tell the world. He'd say, "World, yes, I've done a whole lotta race in my time and I know it's a buncha jumpin' jack flash and it doesn't really help Serious Scholars do Serious Scholarship and in fact it makes us lie about the past and S&S explained it all to me the other day and I get it now. Thanks S&S!"

KM: Oh sure; he'd jump right on it: "World, please buy my books on Paleoindians and listen to my papers on Paleoindians and… oh, wait a minute, World, I take it all back. All that race stuff in all my books and papers. Never mind!" Sure. Face up, S&S, they'll nevermind you away into racial reservationland forever, or at least as long as archaeologists all feel comfortable making you into a loyal Indian when they get together to talk over things in their books.

S&S: Maybe you're right, Kennewickman. I wouldn't even get a crust of bread from Meltzer. And I guess I don't really mind. It's not a *quid pro quo* thing for me, like "I'll take you seriously only if you take me seriously." I feel pleased to have Meltzer's book in my office; thanks for writing it, David J. Meltzer—endnotes & all!

KM: Anyway S&S, there's nothing wrong with finding yourself in an endnote. You do that all the time to one person or another, and you don't intend to dismiss them.

S&S: I... I see what you mean, Kennewickman. Why, in my David Meltzer Serious-Science-Like-Endnote I looked around and I happened to see Chicken Nuggets. He got neverminded there too. And then I noticed Egg White and Greasy Chicken. And we stood together, all of us looking around as if we had just peopled a new world but it somehow didn't really matter in David Meltzer's my-expertise-lies-elsewhere version of the story.

KM: Good company. For years all the Chickens have very patiently put up with you in your cross-fire hurricane, S&S. It means something. Even if I don't quite know what.

S&S: Yes, Kennewickman! So I said to them, "Hey there all you almost-Monboddoed almost-half-humaned almost-semi-beasted nativeamericaned Chickens in your stormy place—maybe it's all right now!"

KM: While you stood there, S&S, in your David Meltzer endnote... well, I was drowned. Everyone left me for dead. And when I finally washed up, race drove a spike right through my head.

S&S: I know, Kennewickman. I know! And I... and I howled! "In fact," I said... in that David Meltzer endnote I said to everyone, "Yeah!yeah!yeah! So hey Chickendians, I guess it's gonna be all right! As a matter of fact, it's—"

KM: Yeah, S&S! Isn't it a gas!

I Peer Into Chicken Noodle's Mirror

So it wasn't very long after the end of the second millennium of the Common Era that the fabled Closet Chickens appeared. They took comfort in one another as they faced the end of that time and the beginning of something else. In their vision of the future, in the something-else that would follow, I saw that the Chickens would begin by enacting race. But it would have a new face: "indigeneity."

Chickenry would together embark into a future in which archaeology would learn to become indigenous. The Chickens would decolonize archaeology and remove it from the exclusive control of oppressive and insensitive white colonizers. Indians would empower themselves as a race. Toward this end the Chickens would help each other and their chatter would be heartening as they went forth to perform their almost impossible feats in the world, battling injustice, empowering Native racialism, creating indigenous archaeology; studying the details under the surface, layer after layer . . . lifting up a corner of the earth to see the past, to change the future.

It would be serious work indeed. But they would also laugh together and be supportive and warm in their Coop. For the Coop would change the status quo into something positive. And if they couldn't change the world, they could at least enhance what they liked about it.

And the Chickens would do race, yes. They understood that race had a serious flaw, a serious problem: it told a lie about the nature of humankind. They heard the news about race but could not stop themselves and they went on doing it anyway. And this seemed good to them, something good to aim at. This was the essence of their dream.

Full of hope they were; for they were the Closet Chickens.

When the next millennium opened for business, I stepped inside of it and entered the Coop. Pausing to think of the Closet Chickens, I often smiled to myself. Their optimism and enthusiastic idealism felt good to me. I listened to them and they . . . some of them listened to me.

In the warmth of the Closet Chicken Coop I shared the glow of it, even though I didn't share their vision of things. As I saw it, the fundamental logic of the Coop rested on acceptance of biological racialism. Wasn't this a problem? I thought so.

Maybe other archaeologists and anthropologists accepted the practice of race and race was just something that everybody did. Maybe race had always been done that way in American archaeology and in the academic community and throughout the American world, and maybe even beyond in the wider universe. And maybe the Chickens would do it like that too.

But we didn't necessarily have to do the things of race the same way everyone else did those things. We could do it differently. Standing just inside the entrance of the twenty-first century, I began to consider what to recalibrate.

During the twentieth century the idea of race as an explanation of human biological diversity had been rejected by academic anthropology. For some reason, however, race hadn't died in the academy. It was still going strong in the next millennium. It had given rise to the Closet Chickens. What would we do with it?

Maybe the Coop could be different. We didn't have to do the kind of archaeology and anthropology that had characterized and filled the twentieth century. Maybe we could help each other figure out what to do with race—things that I would never think of by myself. I appreciated their chatter. I stood inside their magic circle and asked for their help.

The Coop seemed an opportune place to play with ideas and implications. Whatever response Chickenry might have to my thoughts, I needed a place to experiment with saying things about race that might sound wise or foolish or both.

Speaking my mind, I felt surprised at first when I realized that the Chickens intended to just proceed anyway with race as their unquestioned bond. Race would define the Coop. The Chickens would enact racially based indigeneity, racially based nativeness, racially based Indianness.

Even so, feeling my way into the beginning of the millennium, the Coop seemed full of hope, and I found myself thinking that whatever came next in my life, maybe I could do it among these archaeologists. Standing among the Chickens, I didn't feel homeless. However they might feel about what I said, they would listen—I often got the impression that many of them had rather complicated responses to the things I said.

Excavating myself to look for the inward meanings of selfhood and racial identity, I wasn't an archaeologist, so it was necessarily a somewhat clumsy enterprise. I must have looked like a looted city in those days. As the Coop arose and made itself in the image of race, I reminded myself that it hadn't been easy for me to question and challenge race in my life. Race is profoundly personal. People don't usually want advice about profoundly personal matters like racial identity even when they ask for it, and no one had asked me for any advice.

All the Chickens had things they wanted to say in the Coop. Important things. Whether or not any of the other Chickens ever took up the challenge of confronting race with me, it would be interesting to hear their chatter. In those first years of the Coop, I tried to say things that mattered, but did I know what mattered?

I had to keep trying to figure it out because race is fundamentally damaging to our humanity. It distorts the nature of humankind. This is a profound truth about racial identity. It does not reveal to us a mirror-image of ourselves; instead it distorts what can be seen and the stories we tell about what we think we see.

We should reject race. If this option does not yet seem a realistic choice for most people, we can at least learn to treat race as culture.

Race doesn't dwell in our physical selves; it sits deep inside the more mysterious workings of our minds. Knowing that race is not an inherent manifestation of the physical self, we must redefine the whole elaborate social structure of racialism as a purely social artifact. Race is a set of malleable guidelines, not a rigid biological reality.

Detached from the anchor of biology, we should recalibrate race into cultural ethnicity. And if we treat race as a form of ethnicity, then racial identities become optional for everyone. This outcome is inevitable because when we free race from the illogic of pseudobiology, we must also drop the associated biological authenticity tests. Liberating ourselves from pseudobiology, we can treat racial identities as self-empowering options subject only to the exercise of personal preference.

This mode of race might well perpetuate racialism, but it is at least an inclusively integrative cultural alternative to the traditional practice of race as a set of exclusively segregated identity structures. Redeploying race into pure ethnicity, we free ourselves to acknowledge that all Americans have absorbed varying amounts of cultural racial identities of every color. Everyone has absorbed racial Indianhood in varying degrees; everyone has more than a few drops of black culture; everyone has some cultural Hispanicness and Asianness and whiteness.

This recalibration of race would put an end to racism because we would be encouraged to take open pride in our mutual ethnic Indianness, our mutual ethnic blackness, the manifold complexity of ethnicity as pure culture. Taking pride together like this, it would soon become impossible to practice racism.

Treating racial identities as optional for everyone, as cultural ethnicity available to everyone—treating race as an inherently inclusive outcome of culture, not biology, this strategy would undermine the exclusive preferential ranking of racism because the practice of bioracialism is the basic ingredient necessary for the practice of racism. Truly hoping to defeat racism forever, we must defeat race itself. In defeating race, let it be seen for what it really is and for what it has actually always been: flexible ethnicity hidden under inflexible pseudobiology. Liberated from racial biology, we can negotiate all we might wish across the complicated terrain of ethnicity and personal identity.

If we wish, we really can choose to give up race.

☙

Thinking such things at the beginning of the twenty-first century, I stood up in the Coop and spoke to the Closet Chickens. Whatever I said or didn't say, I said things the way you say them with your heart. The Closet Chickens paused in their doings and listened.

I said, *Let us free ourselves and be free.*

We'll be free, I said, *Free at last.*

I kept saying things like this. It was an exciting time for the Closet Chickens at the beginning of the third millennium of the Common Era. I loved the warmth of their excitement and their enthusiastic idealism.

I glimpsed them as they spoke to one another in their communal Coop. And they went here & there upon their errands, doing all the things they did. They held their celebrations on alluring green islands. They convened to consider the underlying truths they sought, the deeper mysteries adrift inside the world. They gave names and took them. They were determined, wise, proud.

I stood elsewhere upon my paths in the world and often heard rumor of their mysterious doings. I saw that they didn't want to come with me on my journey. Even so, some of them listened to everything I said. And no one knew what to do about it and it wasn't easy.

I feel sad when I think of this. And I feel happy, too.

Let us feel foolish and wise and sad and happy.

Let us feel free to feel free.

And they listened upon their pathways in real time. And upon my twilight path oblique to theirs, upon my path in imaginary time, I watched them as they set forth to make a difference, as they saw it, a good difference.

For they were the Closet Chickens.

7

In the Ninth Dream

O nce upon a timeless forever morning, long ago in my youth in the millennium that came before this one, I had what I call my "fourth bear dream"—the fourth of seven dreams. In this dream, there were important things I needed to learn and I was lucky.

I had just enough time to hide among the shadowy rafters before they arrived. They entered through the door, arriving singly and in little groups until the wooden walls of the secret cabin in the forest seemed to bulge with the breathing of their dense shaggy bodies.

The door closed.

I watched as their low growling voices below brought them together, moving and swaying in a peculiar circuit, their magic circle. Hours passed in this fashion.

In the deep night I became aware that they were talking about me, discussing what must be done. Occasionally one or several would pause and peer up at me as I crouched among the rafters. I felt glad to be so high up in the unlit darkness.

It took them all night to decide what must be done.

In the late spring of 2005 I awoke from a very vivid dream—another bear dream. In this dream I walked on Colfax Avenue in Denver with the woman who filled my position at the Denver Art Museum after I left in 2003.

This woman held certain mysterious objects in her hands. With these things she sought to summon and reveal a magic invisible bear who dwelt in the city. And I could somehow sense the history of the objects in her hands as she wielded them. It was like pausing for a few seconds in the memory of having watched a movie.

Once upon another long-lost time, those objects had been discarded by a kindly old man at her Pueblo, but had been retrieved by a Pawnee who happened to live there. The old man had decided that no one cared about his miraculous implements, his treasures. In his grief he didn't bother to properly retire them. He just threw them away even though it was like throwing away his hands and his heart.

Observing this, the Pawnee felt sad. So he had gone forth to rescue the forsaken items, thinking they'd find a place of honor elsewhere in a future that the old man couldn't foresee. The old man had a gentle soul and he would die soon. But maybe he would someday feel grateful as he stood watching the unknown future unfold, watching from the other side. He'd see how the implements would remind everyone of his life and the good things in his heart.

The old man's precious things had finally ended up at the Denver Art Museum. And arriving there several years after the turn of the century, the woman who took my place had been astonished to see the long-lost items and she'd taken care to get instructions on what to do with them.

She wielded them now to summon this magic invisible bear. And she had asked for my help and I had agreed, though it wasn't clear exactly why she needed me. I thought to myself how she must be a very generous person to include me in such special doings.

The magic bear dwelt unseen in the city. No one knew of the bear, but for the sake of the miraculous implements from the museum, the bear would reveal himself in fulfillment of some profound purpose.

I had nothing to do with it, whatever the bear intended. I would simply try to help the new curator, knowing nothing of her task. The two of us walked through the city looking for the bear.

I nodded, "There he is!" I observed the bear walking near my parked car.

My job here was over, so now I'd go home. I had to pass the magic bear to get to my car and I felt relieved to note how he ignored me. He seemed like a very solemn bear. Catching the edge of the bear's aura, I thought I sensed a sometimes-gruff wisdom, a deep integrity, a resilient air.

I grew curious, standing next to my car watching the scene. It was a sunless afternoon in the dream. The dark daylight had been sinking all around us. It had turned into the kind of late afternoon that you don't often see in the city. It felt like the kind of day that you would expect to find hidden at the roots of murky trees in the depths of an ancient shadowy forest. I stood upon the path, listening.

What could they be saying to one another?

The woman spoke softly to the bear on the street corner as I approached. I don't know what he replied to her, but I caught the final comment. The bear murmured: "I've designated a minute for you and thirty minutes for him, so leave us now."

The bear and I slowly walked west down the sidewalk along Colfax. He knew all about how I'd dreamt of bears over the preceding thirty years—in fact, hadn't that same bear attended the ceremony that I had dreamed of in my youth? The ceremony in my fourth bear dream. Maybe this was another visit to help me do whatever I had to do next.

I told the bear everything that had happened to me in my job in Denver at the Colorado Historical Society and at the Denver Art Museum. I spoke about my colleagues and the people I'd dealt with—how we had all tried to do important things, hoping to make a difference, and how all of us had poured our hearts into what we did, and how I had finally moved on.

I feel glad about what I did in those days, but there were lonely moments for me in the things that happened. People who should have aided me chose otherwise. Occasionally I had to do alone some of the important things that needed to be done. Whatever happened then, I knew that no one would ever care about what had happened to me the way this bear would care.

Absorbing my story, hearing the truth behind my words, the bear offered some advice. If a bear ever bothers to speak to you in a dream, I'm sure you'll listen even if you don't completely understand.

"I want you to do one thing."

As I stood there ready to hear what that one thing might be, a realization came over me like another movie flashback. When this bear spoke, his words would fulfill the purpose of this part of his enchanted life. In that moment on the street, the old invisible bear would at last make manifest and discharge a weighty duty, a strange fate laid upon him long ago in a mysterious conclave—the mystical fulfillment of the ceremony in my fourth bear dream. After this the bear would move on to the next thing in his life as if thirty years of invisibility in this city were a humble and unremarkable sacrifice, a true gift.

The bear was brusque. But somehow the exact words only vaguely matched what the bear really said. Beneath the surfaces of his words I heard a sense of warmth and knowingness, a bestowing of peace, a wise kindliness of spirit for hands and hearts. Such things seem impossible to explain.

"Stop saying 'we' when you speak of what happened to you."

And once upon a timeless forever afternoon, later on at the end of that same summer in the land of rangers and bears and Hispanics and questions that can't be answered, a very special feeling came upon me one day.

I walked in the forest with my wife Linda. We stood on a shady curving pathway among evergreens and I can't explain it. Maybe it felt something like the memory of rain and the memory of thunder. A drenched moment inside a dream as I stood there, a lucid dream.

Perhaps the forward momentum of our stressful daily lives obscures it, making us stoop slightly inside. But that feeling must always be somewhere just beneath our surfaces, a far-off green music that slips beneath the trees along the path.

I stood there next to Linda that afternoon in the leafy shade and enjoyed it. Shall we float, dear friend, as if floating upon vast pools of long-lost poetry?

The serene quantum curvatures that flow in and out of the past and future help us to weave the strands of our stories together in many ways, each pattern a different trip, yet somehow the same journey. In the hidden wayfaring that fills our sleep, echoing in the waking world, the words are the same, but they mean something quite variable, contingent, fateful, beautiful.

8

In the Land of Rangers and Bears and Hispanics

W hen I'm not off hiking along the foothills and mountains and greenways of Colorado, I sometimes wander around the wwweb. In early 2005, for example, I began to follow breaking news about Ward Churchill, a pro-race ethnic studies professor who came under media scrutiny for writing an unpopular and insensitive commentary on the 9/11 attacks against the United States. I got interested in this case while pondering the distinctions in our public discourse between "race" and "ethnicity."

Pushed into mounting a due-process witch-hunt against Churchill, the University of Colorado eventually found him guilty of having committed various unpopular academic felonies in some of his writings, and they tied him to a stake and fired him in July 2007. Churchill apparently exaggerated and fabricated a few things and he broke several other rules of scholarship, and he made it a regular habit to write about Indians and white people as if race were a biological reality.

But he wasn't fired for fomenting race in a big way. No.

Ward Churchill's racialized social commentary—a typical American narrative full of the typical tall tales told by race—proved to be unremarkable among even his most determined detractors. The doing of race is a popular thing for an academician to do, whether sensitively or not.

Other aspects of this tale also proved weirdly strange and weirdly commonplace. You see, most Americans questioned Churchill's politics, but most racial Indians questioned his asserted Indian racial identity. Commenting in July 2007 to reporter Gale Courey Toensing of the race-based newspaper *Indian Country Today*, James Riding In decried the problem of "ethnic fraud." A leading pro-race scholar of academic Indian studies, Riding In was not alone in raising this concern.

Another prominent adherent to racial Indianhood, Suzan Shown Harjo, soon followed with similar sentiments in a column in *Indian Country Today*. Complaining about CU's policy of accepting self-identification of racial identity at face-value, she wondered, "What makes you think Ward Churchill is a Native person?"

It is interesting to note how Harjo's point about racial identity seemed intended to cover the same space in public meaning as Riding In's point about "ethnic" fraud. In fact, the terms "race" and "ethnicity" typically display a quite companionable presence in American public discourse. They often stand together beneath the public spotlight, side-by-side in usage. I listen closely for some indication of distinction between the two terms, and at times it does appear that people intend differing meanings, but most often the words convey an air of amiable interchangeability.

Sometimes you say race; sometimes ethnicity.

I sometimes wonder whether this blurring of the line between the two terms might reflect the fact that race has been discredited as a useful way to characterize humankind. But no. "Ethnicity" seems to be comfortably settling in as just another aspect of race, or perhaps even as the new face of race, as if its meaning might well derive from the permanent and rigid laws of genetic heritability rather than from the permeable and flexible guidelines of culture.

This prospect is worrisome because ethnicity is what people experience through processes of culture, while race presumes to be a rigid biological description of humankind. In the academy, most scholars know that race has died as a scientific explanation of human physical diversity. But it would be pointless to look for evidence of the death of race in American lifeways. The signs are few indeed. And it appears that dead race is not being replaced by living ethnicity. Instead, racialism seems to have overwhelmed ethnicity, emptying it of independent meaning and filling it up with the intentions of race. Race is dead, but rather than do the necessary work to come up with another world, we've merely come up with another word.

I often wonder what a non-racial "another world" might look like. I peer beyond the grave of racialism, looking for what will come next. I don't know what to expect on the other side of race, but every so often I think I do catch glimpses of the world that will follow the world of race. In pursuit of this elusive future, I made an interesting discovery about myself in the early summer of 2005.

৩৯

Forsaking the internet one afternoon, I took a hike in the mountains under towering thunderclouds with my wife Linda. At the end of the path, crossing a narrow rustic bridge over a creek that tumbled toward the end of the day, a park ranger waved at us.

I didn't want to stop. Earlier, heading up the winding path, I'd seen the questionnaire in her hand. Another ranger stood nearby with a captive couple, writing earnestly on a clipboard. "Let's say no and keep going," I suggested. But Linda was in a good mood and didn't mind stopping.

"Would you mind taking a few minutes to help me with this questionnaire?"

"Okay," said Linda to the ranger, flashing a friendly smile.

The ranger stood before us, her clipboard poised for action. This was official Park business but she nevertheless expected a rebuff, polite or otherwise. The clipboard, if needed, would thwart the worst vibes.

Studying her face, I thought she might be older than us, and it was late in the day and she looked tense and tired. Maybe she'd been counting bears all day in the forest and they hadn't been very cooperative.

It was a lengthy questionnaire. Beginning with "What did you enjoy about the park?" and working on down to the punchline: "Would you be willing to pay more in entrance fees?" Linda answered carefully, as if sworn in. I stood nearby, trying not to look like I might turn rude at any moment, another surly bear. I watched as the ranger checked off each query.

"What race are you?" She turned away from Linda and looked at me, shaking me out of my reverie.

I'd been pondering what to say when she got to the question about race, running over some possible responses. I knew Linda would want me to keep it simple. I usually do. It seems rude when chatting casually with people to blow up all their ideas about race in the midst of a few pleasantries. What would I say this time? Was this a casual conversation? Or was it official business?

I couldn't decide and I didn't really want to be rude. "What do you think, Linda?" I'd leave the whole thing to her.

But either there's not much to say, or there's too much. "I don't know," she said, echoing my indecision. "Go ahead and tell her if you want!"

Now I had Linda's permission. I could go after this ranger's expectations and blow away everything she thought about race if I wished. I stroked my chin, picturing how it would go. But it was hopeless. I threw up my hands like a bear standing up to growl at the sun. "Let's just not answer that one!"

"Okay," Linda laughed.

"We don't have an answer for that, so let's skip it."

This was just what the ranger had expected and she felt very clever because she had indeed read us right. She expected us to treat her like a door-to-door sales rep. But the conversation had gotten weird in an unusual and mysterious way.

Okay. She had faced worse; she would persevere. There were bears in this forest that could turn your bones to water with their fearsome charging answers to questions. This was nothing!

No choice, she wrote. She had been prepared to check a square and it was a little inconvenient because now she had to write something that couldn't be readily compiled—where would this go in the carefully gathered and sorted statistics that would provide the science behind the coming increase in park fees?

"Okay. Are you Hispanic? That's ethnicity, not race!" Her lips pursed with satisfaction. The ranger had countered my vaguely emotional tone with her sense of logic. This war could be won. We'll get those bears counted no matter what!

Relenting, I watched her win. It's nice to see people win; I like the look in their eyes. The ranger tapped the clipboard with her pencil to drive home certain incontestable finalities, a victorious glint in her eyes.

On that note, we finished the interview and she let us go.

☉☉

But something very complex also happened. Every so often in the days and weeks and months that followed, I paused with whatever I was doing to think about ethnicity and the idea of being Hispanic.

Am I Hispanic?

The ranger had distinguished race from ethnicity; in her mind the two were not the same thing—maybe her use implied that "Hispanic" could avoid being biologically racial. Maybe it could be strictly a cultural construction.

But how can I not be Hispanic if it is purely cultural, a matter of experience, not biology? Standing there at the end of the path observing the ranger as she finished up with her random survey of visitors to the park, I thought back to my youth.

During the 1960s, when the park ranger was also young, I dwelt upon the Enchanted Isle with my family. I swam in the living sea and I dipped my hands into the bubbling sand and I listened to the ever-present humid trade winds and to the surf like wind in a sunken undersea forest. Upon green seaweed pathways I wandered. And I dearly loved eating the national dish of that far-off realm. I miss it even today. Maybe there's a hollow place inside me that will never be filled.

How could I not be Hispanic after that?

In the Land of Enchantment in 1972 I saw a film about the unforgettable poetry of Pablo Neruda and he became my favorite poet through the years that followed. *No Hay Olvido.* . . . Okay Pablo; go ahead and keep murmuring your sad, beautiful sonata. But sometimes memory is short. Forgetting is long.

Who am I after all these years?

You see, if ethnicity is not race, if ethnicity is a cultural reality that is truly not biologically determined, then the rules of culture have the final say over the character of ethnic identity. According to this logic, we must acknowledge that the idea of being Hispanic comes not from genes, but from exposure to culture.

One can argue that very few Americans, if any, can truthfully assert the total absence of Hispanic cultural ethnicity. To assert that some of us may not be Hispanic is to deny the seeping soaking fluidity of culture. It gets everywhere in your world. You just can't keep it out of all your little nooks and crannies. And once it's there, you can't get rid of it. Pablo Neruda and rice & beans and the Land of Enchantment and the Enchanted Island cannot be made to vanish from my soul.

Embracing this mode of communal Hispanicness means turning aside from the false idea that race is genetic. We would defeat the idea that ethnicity should be like race, suborned by racialism into being pseudobiological rather than the cultural thing it really is.

If ethnicity is truly race-free, then it is a word that usefully evokes the vast complexity and infinitely meaningful details of our cultural selves. We can enrich ourselves constantly through our cultural experiences, and the experience of cultural diversity can give us many ways of being ourselves. We need this kind of ethnicity at the center of our discussions about identity and culture. With race-free ethnicity in hand, we can fill up the old oppressive usages of race with new usages—we can empower ourselves with liberating choices.

ର

Working my way slowly through this logic, thinking back to the ranger's survey, I finally concluded that I must be Hispanic. I am Hispanic if we do not artificially warp the concept of ethnicity with misplaced racial biology. Setting aside the biological imperatives that define the practice of race, the outcome is clear for ethnicity. We must identify ourselves according to our cultural experiences.

Having learned something interesting about myself, I wanted to go back to the eaves of that forest and speak again to the ranger and her clipboard. Maybe I shouldn't have let her win. Maybe I should have flung out my paws to maul her gnarled conception of things.

ର

Returning to the internet several years later in 2007, I glimpsed online the news of Ward Churchill's firing by the University of Colorado. Invited by the media to cast my vote on his doings, I indeed found it reprehensible for him to engage in unapologetic distortions of history and scholarship.

Adherents to racial Indianhood commonly bond by engaging in social criticism of white people, and sometimes they bond by openly indulging in anti-white hostility—an outcome of the fact that plenty of anti-Indian white racism exists in the historical record. To engage in exaggeration and fabrication of evidence, as Churchill was convicted of doing, is to gratuitously manipulate and enflame this racial resentment.

More to the point of my anti-race perspective, whatever the quality of Churchill's erudition and his creative massaging of the master narrative of racial Indianhood, I do not approve of the way that academic scholarship in general deliberately engages in the distortion of our communal identity systems by promoting and sanctioning bioracialism based on long-discredited pseudoscience. By any measure, Ward Churchill's "indigenist" scholarship is predicated squarely upon the two primary tenets of racial Indianhood: advocacy for submission to the dictates of personal bioracial identity, and advocacy for the continued perpetuation of a formal bioracial identity system in the American social world.

Studying this situation here at the beginning of the twenty-first century, I take note of how faithful observance of these tenets of racial Indianhood prevails throughout the academy. In firing Churchill in 2007, CU expressed no qualms about his reliance on racial identity or his advocacy on behalf of race. I have the impression that CU's silence is not innocent—it surely reflects traditional academic protocol in which the doing of race is met with collegial encouragement.

From my perspective, it is impossible to distinguish the racial ideological essentialism of CU from that of Ward Churchill. As I see it, to enter the academic community is to enter into a specific social compact regarding race, and membership in the academy uniformly requires acceptance of at least three assumptions that serve as the basic ingredients of racial practice.

First, people deemed to be racially white are expected to refrain from enacting racial whiteness as a bonding experience. In academic culture, overt racial bonding is treated as a good idea for non-whites, but it is not viewed as socially healthy for whites. In Ward Churchill's case, he would have been burned at the academic stake well before 2007 had he chosen to regularly and explicitly bond with white colleagues through racial whiteness.

Second, non-white people are expected to have functioning racial identities, and they are expected to uniformly treasure and enact their racial identities. Adhering to the identity systems of racial Indianhood, Churchill was regularly rewarded by the University of Colorado for engaging in Indian racial bonding activities.

Finally, race-based intellectual productions are desirable so long as one is not producing and advancing white racialism. People identified as racially white are expected to overtly practice racial whiteness only when requested to do so for the benefit of the practice of non-white racialism. In fact, all members of the academic community are expected to actively facilitate the enactment and affirmation of non-white forms of race and racial bonding.

In other words, Churchill's colleagues were generally expected to have, at minimum, a supportive indifference toward Churchill's professional Indian bonding activities. But CU wasn't supportively indifferent to Churchill's racialism. An ardent Indian indigenist, Churchill ended up as the chair of his department; I can hardly believe that an equally ardent adherent to racial whiteness would have risen to chair a CU department.

As a general matter, there is no such thing as a non-racial cultural option in the academic community. There are plenty of academics for whom the pleasures of racial bonding are anathema, but somehow they still prefer to hear everyone sing the anthems of praise-worthy racialism. We apparently need a social world in which everyone is forced to participate in the production of American racialism.

ೲ

For the near future, the academy may not provide much help in creating the kind of non-racial social option I wish for, but perhaps we can aim at changing the doing of race. Toward this end, I favor replacing the assumptions of race with the assumptions of ethnicity—ethnicity free of bioracialism. With this logic in hand, I do have something in common with the University of Colorado. Like CU, I accept Churchill's self-description as an Indian. He doesn't need any "Indian blood" or citizenship in any racially defined "Indian tribe" to claim an Indian cultural identity.

Unlike CU, however, I think it is inherently anti-academic to permit practitioners of race to force their racialist views on unheeding generations of students. It is wrong to validate the discredited assumptions of race by indulging Churchillian pro-race advocacy, treating such advocacy as intellectually equivalent to the critical study of racialism.

CU must eventually develop policies that take a neutral stance on the culture of race. Academia must neither affirm race in a misguided anti-science way, nor oppose the ability of people to practice treasured belief systems. But in the end, the viability of our intellectual culture must draw its essential vitality from notions that respect the outcomes of scientific knowledge, and the culture of racialism does not respect science-based scholarship. The most logical way for universities to recalibrate racial practice would be for them to learn to see race as a cultural belief system, not a biological truth, and to redefine race as ethnicity.

And treating racial ideology as the belief system that it is, this logical approach to race would lead to a very different kind of academic social contract. Discarding pseudobiological authenticity tests and academic authentication for bioracialism, entrenched artifacts of racial culture like racial Indianhood and racial Hispanicness would inevitably become impossible to define and defend. These and other manifestations of racial identity would gradually slip away into a future without race.

But in 2007, speaking unknowingly at the beginning of the end of race, pro-race racial Indians announced their allegiance to a more traditional American racial culture by characterizing Ward Churchill as a spurious Indian, a wannabe. As Dr. James Riding In observed to reporter Gale Toensing, academically accredited philosophers of Indian studies worried about the presence of "non-Indian cheaters" in their midst—"cheaters" who might actually be racial white people posing as racial Indians. As I saw it, however, it seemed patently evident that ethnic practitioners of cultural Indianhood like Ward Churchill simply stood accused of lacking phony genetic credentials for their asserted Indian identities.

And it is race itself that is phony.

☉☉

With this logic in hand, we must inevitably wander down a particular path that is presently little-traveled. Since race represents a perversion of the nature of humankind, it seems proper to conclude that scholarship which unquestioningly enacts bioracialism must be phony. In addition, when this phony scholarship treats adherents to racial Indianhood as inherently biologically racial, such treatment is inherently dehumanizing.

This insight has important unacknowledged implications for twenty-first century proponents of academic Indian studies and ethnic studies programs. The traditional academic embrace of race creates a profound problem for historical storytelling and for our sense of historical self-awareness. For this reason, it is qualitatively different to study the doings of adherents to racial Indianhood, as opposed to studying the doings of Indians. Knowing that race deforms both humankind and human history, it seems logical to suggest that the social construction of race as a biological truth needs useful study rather than uncritical perpetuation.

When scholarship proceeds on the basis of assuming that race is a valid biological interpretation of humankind, and when scholars of race engage in the admitted practice of the lie of racialism. . . . Well, for the moment, no university treats the unabashed promotion of bioracial discourse as a problem. No university thinks it useful to challenge or interfere in any way with the ability of racialists to pass along intact the delusion of race.

Listing Ward Churchill's crimes against the academy, no one thought it pertinent to challenge Ward Churchill's credentials on the basis of his agenda of openly propagandizing and proselytizing on behalf of the bogus idea of race.

Studying the situation through an analytical lens, we see James Riding In and Ward Churchill (and Suzan Shown Harjo) as sibling proponents of American racialism. In their disagreements, they act as if they have espoused conflicting cultural ideologies, but this is an illusion. The pseudobiological sap of race runs true in their veins. Their debate-like arguments represent minor matters of spirited internecine competition, a heated sibling rivalry. In reality, they have together labored mightily to advance the great American enterprise of passing along the precepts of race to future generations.

In 2007 their efforts seemed very successful. Their success in this shared enterprise came with the full blessing and support of the American academic community. Rather than subjecting openly racialist scholars to thorough scrutiny for perpetrating outmoded pseudoscience, and rather than challenging self-professed open purveyors of popular disinformation about the nature of humankind, the academy instead began the twenty-first century by rewarding such scholars with degrees, professorships, and promotions. At the time Ward Churchill became embroiled in controversy, he burst into American consciousness as the chair of an academic department, richly rewarded for his approach to race.

The academy has a responsibility to rethink race studies. We have an urgent need for conscientious specialists in "Indian studies" to lead the way in reconfiguring the study of racial Indianhood in light of the realities of race. This means giving people useful insights into the status of racial Indianhood as a social construction that doesn't deserve its sustaining biological underpinnings. It seems decidedly unscholarly to conduct business as usual, or to quietly claim to be doing race as pure culture without deliberately calibrating into this practice the implications of what this change in status might mean.

Students should beware of scholarship on race that has the expectation of unquestioning acceptance of explicit or implicit biological justifications for racial belief systems. Scholars who deem it of little consequence to promote a major falsehood deserve credibility problems, and such scholars must be expected to shoulder an extra burden to show why their scholarship is to be trusted.

In fact, twenty-first century scholars who make race a topic of professional discourse should hesitate to practice race. The open and unabashed practice of race by credentialed scholars automatically implies a somewhat doubtful commitment to following the logic of an evidence-based process.

It is certainly possible for racialists to teach the true nature of race, just as it is possible for religious biologists to teach evolution in a responsible manner. If committed astrologers were to somehow become entrusted with teaching academic astronomy, we would rightly expect them to strictly separate their private beliefs from their public professorial responsibilities. We do not look for modern-day alchemists to serve as credentialed academic interpreters of chemistry. No university would countenance a women's studies program that has as its explicit agenda the fostering of a nineteenth century acceptance of female intellectual inferiority.

But we place students in the hands of professed racialists every day. The modern academy is rife with historians and anthropologists and sociologists and law professors who have as their express intention the purveying of un-nuanced race-based interpretations of humankind and human history.

When an individual makes an informed choice to engage in the practice of race, this choice must be respected and accommodated. Race-practitioners should not be persecuted for their faith-based beliefs, nor should the academic community police the freely chosen belief-systems of its citizenry. But universities should decline to act as deliberate peddlers of discredited ideas about humankind.

Despite the recognition in science that race distorts the truth of human biological diversity, the enactment of race continues unabated in the academy. And it is clear to me that the predominant mode of racial practice in the academy relies on discredited biological assumptions to sustain the doing of race.

The cultural ideology of race is a compelling social force because it can be mined for ways to organize human society. People invest themselves wholly in the formation and assertion of racial Indianhood, racial Hispanicness, and other such artifacts of racial culture. But race has no biological justification, and this is an important reality. I have chosen to surrender the superpowers of racial identity. For those of us who have given up race, we must question and reject not only the inner structures of racialism, but also the outward public practices that intend to perpetuate race in our midst.

⊙⊙

Perceiving these awful truths, I laugh at myself for dwelling on the comparatively insignificant matter of one hardworking ranger and her clipboard. And for me to depict bears as pointlessly surly, as vicious... well, it is really grisly race that is heartlessly vicious toward humankind.

Doing race, every racialist has the help of highly educated racialist horribilists who wield their impressive credentials and their awesome social strength to run roughshod over what it means to be human. For the moment, racialism has the power to not only bestow upon its adherents academic success, it also publishes race-based newspapers like *Indian Country Today*, and it creates federally funded surveys that believe in race, and it labors to distort ethnicity into race.

Even so, I have little doubt that someday some of us—and eventually, many of us—will find ways to free ourselves from race. For those who choose to go on doing race: you must expect the rest of us to slowly unshackle ourselves from the inherited chains of racial traditions, the oppressive bonds of racialism.

And being free, I suspect that we will return to the forest a little wiser than when we left it. Permitting race to slip away into ethnicity and on into the graveyard of discredited ideas, in the future we'll get on with more useful pursuits.

I feel certain that in the end we'll get those bears counted no matter what.

9

In the Tenth Dream

In a very pleasant green forest I walked
I saw bears off through the tree-trunks
I turned away. One seemed to follow.
I left the path. Along the river I walked
yes I knew where the bears gathered
yes I would live with them for a time
underwater at the river's edge, safe
I could slip into the river and the water
and the brush and the rock overhang
would keep me safe from the bears &
finally one day among the bears two
coyotes spied me and a bear observed
them sniffing out my hiding place &
after that the bears sought me there
they couldn't see very well with their
heads underwater, just the driftwood
I used to fend them off lightly
day after day and I could hold
my breath for a long time, I could
find clever new air pockets under
the rock overhang, in fact I took
a shovel to the rock and tried to extend
the shelter to make it even safer, but
it collapsed, oh well, I didn't need it
I swam with a she-bear in the deep river
I think she appreciated my company
we swam among the bears like that
but not long later she grabbed hold
and took me down to the river-bottom
wrestling playfully as bears do, wishing
me no harm, but I don't know anymore
I-I'll leave the river of the bears. One
wanted to follow and catch hold of me
as bears do. He followed me on the path.
I hurried. I soon caught up with several
other people at the edge of Kansas City.
Now I stand on a street looking at a map.
I consult with a park ranger. Now I take
my bike down Sixth Street across the city.
Getting on my bicycle I say goodbye
to Linda. She's on her way back in time

to Longmont. I ride on for a while
I decide to board a very crowded bus
the driver must count everyone before
driving the bus around a huge hill
on the other side several stops later almost
everyone gets off. A nude woman sunbathes
nearby & on the other side she steps on board
suddenly wearing clothes. Getting off the bus
I get on my bike again. Soon I'll arrive
at Bill's house in the city. On my way I ride
through a bookstore. I like the thought
of coming back to look at the books, it
would be nice, I think. & Linda appears.
Let's go to Bill's house together, I suggest,
before you set forth in time for Longmont

Index

About the Author

Historian Roger Echo-Hawk is the author of an online book on the origins of racial identity among his Pawnee ancestors: *The Enchanted Mirror: When the Pawnees Became Indians* (2007). He is also the author of *Keepers of Culture: Repatriating Cultural Items Under the Native American Graves Protection and Repatriation Act* (2002, Denver Art Museum) and (with Walter Echo-Hawk) *Battlefields and Burial Grounds: The Indian Struggle to Protect Ancestral Graves in the United States* (1994, Lerner Publications).